The
NATIVE AMERICAN
CRAFTS DIRECTORY
SECOND EDITION

A GUIDE FOR
LOCATING CRAFT SHOPS
AND CRAFT SUPPLIERS

OVER 1000 ENTRIES

Compiled by
Diane L. McAlister
(Standing-On-A-Star Woman)

Book Publishing Company
Summertown, Tennessee

Front cover photo by Lee Marmon
Back cover top photo by Doug McAlister
Cover design by Warren C. Jefferson and Jeffery Clark

Book Publishing Company
P.O. Box 99
Summertown, TN 38483 USA
800-695-2241

ISBN 1-57067-058-7   0 9 8 7 6 5 4 3 2

McAlister, Diane L., 1948-
    The Native American Crafts Directory: A Guide for Locating Craft Shops and Craft
    Suppliers / compiled by Diane L. McAlister (Standing-On-A-Star Woman).—2nd ed.
    p. cm.
    "Over 1000 Entries."
    Includes index.
    ISBN 1 -57067-058-7
    1. Indians of North America—Industries—Directories. 2. Indian Art—North
America—Directories. 3. Indian craft—United States—Directories. I. Title
E98.15M33 1998
381' .45745'08997073—dc21   98-16036
                              CIP

CONTENTS

PREFACE

Compiled by a Native American for Native Americans and those interested in Native Americans, this guide is a comprehensive directory to USA and Canadian businesses, individuals, and tribal reservation enterprises, complete with addresses, telephone numbers, and type of products and services offered.

Whether you're looking for classic Indian art, traditional Native American handcrafted items, contemporary Southwest-style home decor, wholesale Indian craftmaking supplies and beads, American Indian books, or tipis and buffalo robes, this directory will tell you exactly where to find it! This directory is primarily for use by Native Americans who are searching for craft supplies or marketing outlets, and for consumers, buyers and sellers of Native American and Southwest-style art, crafts, and related merchandise and publications.

Native American art and crafts are enjoying tremendous popularity in this decade, perhaps more than ever before. Today's explosion of creative expression by the Indigenous People of the Americas has never been more prolific, more imaginative, more unique, or more beautiful. Both ancient AND contemporary Indian artistry is classic, timeless, and collectible. The unique style of hand crafting that is exquisitely "Indian" is found nowhere else on earth except in the Americas.

Not all products and services listed in the *Native American Crafts Directory* are "Indian-made." Numerous businesses offer replica or "Indian-inspired" crafts and merchandise, which, while not Indian-made, may still be very beautiful and worth purchasing. For instance, rustic wood furniture and contemporary non-Native ceramics, are very popular in Indian homes for ethnic decor. Shop judiciously, if you prefer authentic Indian-made.

The "Indian Arts and Crafts Act of 1990" has made unlawful the misrepresentation of Indian-produced goods and products. It is illegal to offer or display for sale any product that falsely suggests it is Indian-produced, an Indian product, or the product of a particular Indian or Indian Tribe or Indian arts and crafts organization. So, if you're looking for authentic Indian-made products only, ASK the dealer before purchasing.

Native Americans are very protective of certain sacred religious items, such as Plains Pipestone Pipes. There is currently an aggressive movement underway in Indian Country against the display, sale, or purchase of Pipestone "peace pipes," as some people call them. To commercialize the sacred Pipestone Pipe is considered a desecration and exploitation of Native American religious spirituality by many elders and spiritual leaders of Plains Tribes. It is tantamount to the buying and selling of sacred Eagle feathers and other holy relics. It is therefore asked by the author that buyers respect the cultural, spiritual, and moral tenets of the Plains people by not purchasing a Pipestone Pipe.

USING THE *NATIVE AMERICAN CRAFTS DIRECTORY*

For quick reference, the TABLE OF CONTENTS categorizes Native American products and services in twelve major, broad categories. The broad categories are further listed by state. Inside each state listing the cities are entered alphabetically. The index lists businesses by topic and name and directs you to the page where they are listed. Many businesses in the directory may offer a variety of goods or services, but multiple listings do not occur. Listings new for this edition are indicated by an asterisk (*). Abbreviations used are: NA = Native American, SW = Southwest.

Many businesses and individuals listed in the directory request a modest fee for their catalogs, or else a SASE (a long, self-addressed, stamped envelope). If these are requested, please comply. Postage and printing expenses can be enormous for small, grass-roots, family-owned enterprises which cannot afford to freely send out mass catalog mailings to the public. If catalog information is not listed, telephone to see if they have one. The business may not have a catalog. They may offer only "one-of-a-kind" custom merchandise which would make a catalog unfeasible. This is especially true of many small family enterprises and Indian Reservation businesses, whose available goods are constantly rotating, as well as art galleries who may specialize in expensive or rare antique collections and single, unique artifacts. If you wish wholesale information, you will most likely be required to write to the company on your business letterhead.

Fine Art, Galleries, Collectibles, Antiques

ALASKA

* ALASKA IVORY EXCHANGE
700 W 4th Ave
Anchorage
AK 99501-2107
Products: NA arts

* ARTIC ROSE GALLERIES
420 L St
Anchorage
AK 99501-1937
Products: NA art and crafts

* ARTIQUE LTD
314 G St
Anchorage
AK 99501-2125
Products: NA art and crafts

* ARTWORKS, THE
3677 College Road
Fairbanks, AK 99709-3712
Products: Indian and Eskimo art

* ALASKA INDIAN ARTS INC
No 23 Fort Seward Dr
Haines, AK 99827
Products: NA art

* ALEXANDERS ART CENTER
329 Harbor Dr
Sitka, AK 99835-7554
Products: NA art

* SS PRINCESS CHARLOTTE FINE GIFTS
PO Box 535
Skagway, AK 99840
Products: NA gifts

ARIZONA

* FOURTH WORLD NATIVE AMERICAN ART
PO Box 1442
Camp Verde
AZ 86322-1442
Products: NA art

* DE CHELLY GALLERIES INC
PO Box 1936
Chinle, AZ 86503-1936
Products: NA art

* HOELS INDIAN SHOP
Oak Cr Rt Box 200
Flagstaff, AZ 86001
Products: Native American arts and crafts

* INDIAN COUNTRY
3 E Aspen Ave
Flagstaff, AZ 86001-5220
Products: NA art and merchandise

GRIDLEYS
16830 Avenue of the Fountains
Fountain Hills, AZ 85268
Products: Western art, pen and ink western portraits

SANTA FE EXPRESS
16855 Parkview Ave
Fountain Hills, AZ 85269
602-837-9742
Products: Western art, pen and ink western portraits

* GALLERY AT THE GRAND CANYON
PO Box 3217
Grand Canyon
AZ 86023-3217
Products: NA art, crafts

* MONONGYA GALLERY
PO Box 287
Kykotsmovi, AZ 86039
Products: NA and SW items

* INDIAN JOE ART GALLERY
329 Lake Havasu Ave
Lake Havasu, AZ 86403
Products: NA art

BUDDY TUBINAGHTEWA
PO Box 34321
Phoenix, AZ 85067
602-203-0362
Products: Hopi carvings and paintings

GALLERY OF THE SOUTHWEST
3400 E Sky Harbor Blvd
Phoenix, AZ 85034-4403
Products: NA art

* New listings, NA = Native American,
SW = Southwest.

* JORDAN FINE ARTS AT SOUTH MOUNTAIN
9402 S 43rd Pl
Phoenix, AZ 85044-5545
Products: NA art

* GILA RIVER ARTS & CRAFTS CENTER
PO Box 457
Sacaton, AZ 85247-0457
Products: NA crafts, art, jewelry, merchandise

* FINE APACHE ARTS
PO Box 57
San Carlos
AZ 85550-0057
Products: NA art

* PHILLIP TITLA STUDIO
PO Box 497
San Carlos, AZ 85550-0497
602-526-7143
Info: Send SASE
Products: Wood sculptures and oil paintings

* ARTISTIC GALLERY
7077 E Main
Scottsdale
AZ 85251-4325
Products: NA art

* BUCK SAUNDERS GALLERY
2724 N Scottsdale Rd
Scottsdale, AZ 85257-1349
Products: NA art

GALLERY 10
7045 3rd Ave
Scottsdale, AZ 85251
602-994-0405
Products: NA pottery, baskets, more

GREYTHORNE GALLERY
7103 E Main St
Scottsdale, AZ 85253
602-423-8662
Catalogue: Available
Products: NA items

* LOVENA OHL GALLERY
4251 N Marshall Way
Scottsdale
AZ 85251-3203
602-945-8212
Products: NA arts and crafts

RAWHIDE
PO Box 12966
Scottsdale, AZ 85262
Products: Western art, pen and ink western portraits

* RITA NEALS OLD TERRITORIAL SHOP
7220 E Main St
Scottsdale, AZ 85251-4413
602-945-5432
Products: Specializes in historic Pima, Apache, Hopi and Tohono O'Odham baskets

UNA GALLERY
Scottsdale, AZ
602-423-9160
Products: Ongoing exhibit historic Navajo weavings 1880 to 1940; contemporary folk art

* HONANI CRAFTS
PO Box 221
Second Mesa
AZ 86043-0221
Products: Honani silver jewelry, pottery, paintings, baskets; Navajo rugs; Zuni jewelry

* EL PRADO GALLERIES
PO Box 1849
Sedona, AZ 86339-1849
Products: NA art

* ENGESSERS GALLERY
333 N Hwy 89A Ste 6
Sedona, AZ 86336-4238
Products: NA art

* HUGH PERRY GALLERY
439 Hwy 179
Sedona, AZ 86336-6109
Products: NA art

* JOE WILCOX FINE ARTS
271 N Hwy 89A
Sedona, AZ 86336-4241
Products: NA art, handcrafts

* New listings, NA = Native American, SW = Southwest.

* MANY HANDS GALLERY
PO Box 10089
Sedona, AZ 86339-8089
Products: Indian art, craftworks

* MOUNTAIN TRAILS GALLERY
PO Box 10153
Sedona, AZ 86339-8153
Products: Indian and western art

* MISTY MOUNTAIN GALLERY
PO Box 30001
Tubac, AZ 85646-3001
Products: Indian art

AMERICAS
2841 N Campbell Ave
Tucson, AZ 85719
520-881-6432
Products: Antique North and South American Indian art

BAHTI INDIAN ARTS
4300 Campbell Ave
Tucson, AZ 85718
520-577-0290
Products: Fine Indian arts

MEDICINE MAN ART GALLERY
J Mark Sublette
7000 E Tanque Verde Rd
Tucson, AZ 85715
520-722-7798
Products: Textiles, early-American western art

ARKANSAS

* CHEROKEE MOUNTAIN GALLERY
PO Box 633
Eureka Springs
AR 72632-0633
Products: NA art

* INDIAN PAINTBRUSH GALLERY INC
PO Box 895
Siloam Springs
AR 72761-0895
Products: NA art

CALIFORNIA

B & R ART GALLERY
17720 Sierra Hwy
Canyon Country
CA 91351-1635
800-255-6498
Catalog: Free
SW brochure: Free
Products: NA prints by artists such as Bev Doolit-tle, Maija, Terpning, Gentry Sculptures, jewelry, more

BALLOUES STUDIO
26838 Grandview Ave
Hayward, CA 94542
510-538-4003
Products: Originals and reproductions; artist

* BEAR N COYOTE GALLERY
PO Box 1345
Jamestown
CA 95327-1345
Products: NA art

* BEARCLOUD GALLERY
18500 Rawhide Rd
Jamestown, CA 95327
Products: Indian art; NA items

* SUNBIRD GALLERY
12455 Briones Way
Los Altos
CA 94022-3208
Products: NA art and Indian items

* MARJORIE CAHN GALLERY
PO Box 2065
Los Gatos, CA 95031-2065
408-356-0023
Brochures/photos: Available
Products: NA fine art, bronzes, dolls, textiles, graphics, sculptures Plains quilts, paintings, fine art

* ATLATLE GALLERIES
123 Rheem Blvd
Orinda, CA 94563-3620
Products: NA art, crafts

* ADAGIO GALLERIES
193 S Palm Canyon Dr
Palm Springs
CA 92262-6303
Products: NA art

* COFFMANS FINE ART
457 N Palm Canyon Dr
Palm Springs
CA 92262-5665
Products: NA art

MANY HORSES GALLERY
100 Sunrise Way #460
Palm Springs
CA 92262-6737
Products: NA art and
craft items

TALES OF THE WEST
1233 West Ave P Ste 253
Palmdale, CA 93551
800-497-7401
Products: Relief sculptures, hand painted, wolf
& other wildlife subjects

HANDS GALLERY
175 Pomery Ave
Pismo Boardwalk Mall
Pismo Beach, CA
805-773-8402
Products: Etched rock
art (wildlife and NAs)
by Roberta Miller

* GALLERY OF THE AMERICAN WEST
121 K St
Sacramento
CA 95814-3226
Products: NA art, artifacts

* BAZAAR DEL MUNDO GALLERY
2754 Calhoun St
San Diego
CA 92110-2706
Products: NA art

* AMERICAN INDIAN CONTEMPORARY ARTS GALLERY
685 Market St Ste 250
San Francisco
CA 94105-4200
415-495-7600
No mail order
Products: Contemporary
art, sculpture, SW pottery and jewelry, and
Navajo textiles

* IMAGES OF THE NORTH
1782 Union St
San Francisco
CA 94123-4407
415-673-1273
Catalog: Available
Products: Specializing in
contemporary Inuit art
from Canada and
Alaska

TRIBAL CRAFTS
PO Box 194
San Leandro, CA 94577
510-530-0522
Products: NA art and
sculpture

BOEHM GALLERY
Palomar College
1140 W Mission Rd
San Marcos, CA
619-744-1150 ext 2425
Products: NA exhibits

* CHARLES HECHT GALLERIES
18555 Ventura Blvd
Tarzana, CA 91356-4101
Products: NA art

* KACHINA ART GALLERY
PO Box 4800
Whittier, CA 90607-4800
Products: NA art

* ANSEL ADAMS GALLERY
PO Box 455
Yosemite National Park
CA 95389-0455
Products: Indian art

COLORADO

* BRYNE GETZ GALLERY
PO Box 4737
Aspen, CO 81612-4737
Products: NA art

* New listings, NA = Native American,
SW = Southwest.

CAROL SNOW
PO Box 17787
Boulder, CO 80308-0787
303-499-4513
Products: Wildlife/NA
art, prints, embossings,
paintings

BUCKSKIN JOES
Canon City, CO
719-275-5485
Products: NA art, pen
and ink western portraits

*** EAGLE ROOST
GALLERY**
2803 N Prospect St
Colorado Springs, CO
80907-6324
Products: NA art

*** FLUTE PLAYER
GALLERY**
2501 W Colorado Ave
Colorado Springs
CO 80904-3070
Products: Indian art,
handcrafts

*** MESA VERDE
POTTERY
Gallery Southwest**
PO Box 9
Cortez, CO 81321-0009
800-441-9908
Products: Traditional
pottery, weavings, sil-
verwork

**DAVID COOK FINE
AMERICAN ART**
1637 Wazee St
Denver, CO 80202
303-623-8181
Products: Over 100 tex-
tiles collected from 1975
to the present

*** DENVER ART
MUSEUM GIFT SHOP**
100 W 14th Ave
Denver, CO 80204-2713
Products: NA art, crafts,
merchandise

*** DENVER MUSEUM
OF NATURAL
HISTORY**
2001 Colorado Blvd
Denver, CO 80205-5732
Products: NA art, craft-
work, merchandise,
exhibits

**GALLERY ONE OF
DENVER**
1512 Larimer St
Denver, CO 80202-1610
Products: NA art

*** GALLERY ONE OF
DENVER**
2940 E 2nd Ave
Denver, CO 80206-4904
Products: NA art

*** MUSEUM OF
WESTERN ART**
1727 Tremont Pl
Denver, CO 80202-4006
Products: NA-inspired
art

*** PATH OF THE SUN
IMAGES**
3020 Lowell Ave
Denver, CO 80211-3641
303-477-8442
Price list: Send SASE
Products: Paintings,
sculptures, traditional
and contemporary crafts
and graphic art

* TERMAR GALLERY
780 Main Ave
Durango, CO 81301-5437
Products: NA art

**SOUTHWESTERN
COLLECTION, THE**
6921 Hwy 73
Evergreen, CO 80439
303-670-3290
Products: SW and
mountain style rugs,
jewelry, sculpture, prints,
and original paintings

* FALLIS GALLERY
1412 Patterson Rd
Grand Junction
CO 81506-4019
Products: NA art

HANGMAN
220 Willowbrook Rd
Grand Junction
CO 81505
970-242-2235
Products: Western
framed prints

TWO ELK GALLERY
102 Main St
Minturn, CO
970-827-5307
Products: Western home furnishings

JUST US ORIGINALS
Star Rt Box 508
Pagosa Springs, CO 81447
970-264-4462
Products: Western art

* LONE MOUNTAIN GALLERY
450 E Lions Head Cir
Vail, CO 81657-5228
Products: NA art, craftworks

CONNECTICUT

* RALPH W STURGES
97 Raymond St
New London
CT 06320-3831
203-442-8005
No mail order
Products: Marble carvings: whales, seals, birds, elephants, horses, ships, seascape, landscape

DISTRICT OF COLUMBIA

* FAMCO & NAICA GALLERY
1227 Savannah Ste SE
Washington
DC 20032-4548
202-561-1354
Info: Send SASE
Products: Carvings, pottery, beadwork, sterling silver

FLORIDA

* SUNDANCER GALLERY
6 Florida Ave
Cocoa Village, FL 32922
407-631-0092
Catalog: $2
Products: Artwork, T-shirts, head dresses, jewelry, rugs, crafts, tiles, night lights, lamps, more

* SAGEBRUSH GALLERY
5440 Peppertree Dr
Fort Myers, FL 33908-2136
Products: NA items

* FOUR WINDS GALLERY INC
340 13th Ave S
Naples, FL 33940-7200
Products: NA art, merchandise

* ABORIGINAL ARTS OF THE FIRST PERSON
2340 Periwinkle Way
Sanibel, FL 33957-3221
813-395-2200
Products: Gallery presentations of NA art and crafts

* FOUR WINDS GALLERY
17 Filmore Drive
Sarasota, FL 34236-1425
Products: Native art

GEORGIA

* OGLEWANAGI GALLERY
842 B North Highland Ave
Atlanta, GA 30306
404-872-4213
Bi-annual newsletter
Products: NA crafts, rugs, silver work, pottery, beadwork, drums Newsletter, Indian concerns

SILVER SUN GALLERY
76 Upper Alabama St
Atlanta, GA 30303
404-614-0610
Products: NA art, tribal reproductions, jewelry, rugs, Kachinas

TEKEKWITHA
PO Box 338
Helen, GA 30545
706-878-2938
Products: Na fine arts

* TAFACHADY GALLERY
3282 Mount Pisgah Rd
Ringgold, GA 30736-5942
Products: NA items, art

IDAHO

* GALLERY, THE
507 E Sherman Avenue
Coeur de Alene
ID 83814-2730
208-667-2898
No catalog
Products: Paintings, bronze/paper/marble sculptures, prints, pottery, jewelry, 2000 custom frames

* ANN REED GALLERY
PO Box 597
Ketchum, ID 83340-0597
Products: NA art

ELK DREAMER GALLERY
Rt 1 Box 130
Priest River, ID 83856
208-263-7778
Products: Handcrafted Eagle Talon Knives

PAWEL RACZKA GALLERY
PO Box 674
Sun Valley, ID 83353
208-788-0102
Info: Call
Products: Exhibitions and sales of contemporary N Plains and Plateau NA art

ILLINOIS

* SUNRISE GALLERY
891 Addison Rd
Addison, IL 60101-4858
Products: NA art

* INDIAN ART UNLIMITED
RR 1 Box 283
Carmi, IL 62821-9761
Products: NA art

AMERICAN FRONTIER
Chicago, IL
312-654-8412
Products: Ongoing exhibit of historic art and artifacts including early Plains craftworks

JAN CICERO GALLERY
221W Erie St
Chicago, IL 60610
312-440-1904
Products: Art and crafts of NAs

MONGERSON WUNDERLICH
704 Wells St
Chicago, IL 60610-3510
312-943-2354
Products: NA art, crafts

ALASKA SHOP GALLERY
Chicago, IL
312-943-3393
Products: Presentations of NA artisans

ORCA ART GALLERY
300 W Grand ave
Chicago, IL 60610-4115
312-245-5245
Catalog: Free
Products: Eskimo, Inuit, NW coast tribal art Masks, prints, sculptures, totem poles, more

* TATONKA GALLERY
15136 Willow Ln
Oak Forest, IL 60452-1542
Products: Indian art

* CENTAUR WEST GALLERIES
PO Box 444
Wheaton, IL 60189-0444
Products: NA art

IOWA

ONE FEATHER GALLERY
410 2nd St
Pisgah, IA
712-456-2702
Products: NA art

KANSAS

DON DANE STUDIO
PO Box 2578
Olathe, KS 66063
913-829-3422
Products: Western prints, graphites

LOISIANA

* GALLERY OF THE MESAS
2010 Rapides Ave
Alexandria
LA 71301-6635
318-442-6372
Photos: Available
Products: SW land-
scapes, jewelry, pottery,
kachinas Prints by Pena,
Doug West, Gorman,
Atkinson

MERRIL DOMAS AMERICAN INDIAN ART
324 Chartres St
New Orleans
LA 70116-3223
Products: Indian art

MAINE

* CENTER OF NATIVE ART
RR 3 Box 649
Wiscassett, ME 04578-9412
Products: NA art

* CENTER OF NATIVE ART
RR 1
Woolrich
ME 04579-9801
Products: NA art

MARYLAND

* EARTH ART GALLERY
8600 Foundry St
Savage, MD 20763-9512
Products: NA merchan-
dise

MASSACHUSETTS

HERITAGE ON THE GARDEN, THE
63 Park Plaza
Boston, MA 02116
508-779-6241
Products: Auctions of N
American Indian and
Eskimo art

* INUIT IMAGES
PO Box 2501
Quincy, MA 02269-2501
Products: Alaskan art

MINNESOTA

* MA EN GUN STUDIO GALLERY
5901 Rhode Island Ave N
Crystal, MN 55428-3257
Products: NA artworks

ANCIENT TRADITIONS GALLERY
1010 Nicollet Mall
Minneapolis, MN 55403
612-371-9546
Products: Exhibits of
NA art and crafts

CHRISTOPHER CARDOZO INC
2601 Irving Ave S
Minneapolis, MN 55408
612-377-2252
Products: Edward S
Curtis vintage pho-
tographs

* PLAINS ART MUSEUM
PO Box 2338
Moorhead
MN 56560-2748
Products: NA art, craft
items

MISSISSIPPI

* GRAND VILLAGE MUSEUM SHOP
400 Jeff Davis Blvd
Natchez, MS 39120-5110
Products: NA art, crafts

MISSOURI

* DREAM CATCHER STUDIO AND GALLERY
RR 3 Box 55
Centralia
MO 65240-9160
Products: NA art

* GOMES GALLERY
8001 Forsyth
St Louis, MO 63105
314-725-1808
Products: NA art, rugs,
more

---

* New listings, NA = Native American,
SW = Southwest.

MONTANA

*** LITTLE COYOTE
GALLERY**
PO Box 53
Ashland, MT 59003-0053
Products: NA art

*** WOLF CHIEF
GRAPHICS**
907 Avenue C NW
Great Falls, MT 59404-1731
406-452-4449
Price list: Send SASE
Products: Watercolor
paintings, alabaster and
bronze sculptures, bone
chokers

NEVADA

*** FORTUNATE
EAGLES ROUND
HOUSE GALLERY**
7133 Stillwater Road
Fallon, NV 89406-9034
Products: NA art, crafts

* MALOTTE STUDIO
S Fork Reservation
Star Rt
Lee, NV 89829
702-744-4305
Info: Send SASE
Products: Original
drawings

NEW HAMPSHIRE

*** AMERICAN INDIAN
ARTS**
PO Box 476
Epsom, NH 03234-0476
Products: NA art and
crafts

KOKOPELLI
Wolfeboro Falls, N
603-569-4416
Products: Gallery featuring SW and NA jewelry;
hand-crafted carvings
and fetishes, more

NEW JERSEY

ACQUISITION INC
883 Cooper Landing Rd
#265
Cherry Hill, NJ 08002
609-663-1466
Products: Buyers/deal-
ers of NA items, collec-
tions

**ADOBE EAST
GALLERY**
Summit, NJ
800-24-ADOBE
Products: Presentations
of NA artisans

NEW MEXICO

**COWBOYS AND
INDIANS ANTIQUES**
4000 Central Ave SE
Albuquerque, NM 87108
505-255-4054
Products: American
Indian, cowboy and
frontier material

**ED DEFENDER
STUDIO**
Albuquerque, NM
505-265-0695
Products: Standing Rock
Sioux watercolorist

*** AMERICAN INDIAN
GALLERY**
2034 S Plaza St NW
Albuquerque
NM 87104-1400
Products: NA art

*** JUDY CROSBY
AMERICANA ARTS**
426 Pueblo Solano Rd NW
Albuquerque, NM
87107-6644
Products: NA art

*** SAM ENGLISH
STUDIO GALLERY LTD**
2031 Mountain Rd NW
Bldg C Ste 2
Albuquerque, NM 87104
505-843-9332
Products: Oils, gouach-
es, limited edition reproductions by Ojibwa
artist Sam English

* WILD STRAWBERRY
Muddy Wheel Gallery
4505 4th St NW
Albuquerque, NM 87107
505-345-7671
No catalog
Products: Art of Robert
Kaniatobe, SE fetishes,
necklaces, effigies, head
pots; clay, wood, stone
items

* WRIGHTS INDIAN
COLLECTION
6600 Indian School Rd
Albuquerque
NM 87110-5309
505-883-6122
Products: NA art, jewelry, pottery, storytellers

* ARTIST/DESIGNER
Jerry Ingram
PO Box 428
Corrales, NM 87048-0428
Products: Artist and
designer

DOROTHY
GRANDBOIS
PO Box 2672
Corrales, NM 87048
505-898-3754
Products: Combines
photographic and printmaking talents to create
her Native art

*APACHE MESA
GALLERY & GIFTS
PO Box 233
Dulce, NM 87528-0233
Products: NA art and
crafts

* GALLUP GALLERY
108 W Coal Ave
Gallup, NM 87301-6206
Products: NA art

KIVA GALLERY
200 202 W Hwy 66
Gallup, NM 87301
Products: NA art

* FELIX VIGIL
STUDIO
PO Box 76
Jemez Pueblo, NM 87024
505-834-7772
Products: NA artist

EAGLE MOUNTAIN
FINE ART
PO Box 84
Jemez Springs
NM 87025
505-829-3588
Products: NA artwork,
sculpture, pottery, more

* LINDA LUNDEEN
GALLERY
618 Alameda
Las Cruces, NM 88005
Products: NA art

* FULLER LODGE ART
CENTER
PO Box 790
Los Almos
NM 87544-0790
Products: NA art

EL CERRO GRAPHICS
26 Airport Rd
Los Lunas, NM 87301
505-865-5602
Products: NA art

* COVERED WAGON
GALLERY
2524 Sudderth
Ruidoso
NM 88345-6131
Products: NA art

* MOUNTAIN ARTS
GALLERY
2530 Sudderth Dr
Ruidoso
NM 88345-6131
Products: Indian-
inspired art

ALLAN HOUSER INC
PO Box 5217
Santa Fe, NM 87502
505-471-9667
Products: Sculpture garden, gallery, appraisals,
resales. Representing the
estate of Allan Houser

CHARLES AZBELL
GALLERY
66-70 E San Francisco St
Santa Fe, NM 87501
505-988-1875
Products: NA art, sculpture

* New listings, NA = Native American,
SW = Southwest.

* CONTEMPORARY
SOUTHWEST
GALLERY
123 W Palace Pl
Santa Fe, NM 87501-2045
Products: NA art

* CRISTOFS
106 W San Francisco St
Santa Fe, NM 87501-2112
505-988-9881
Products: Navajo weavings, NA art and crafts

DEWEY GALLERIES
LTD
76 E San Francisco St
Santa Fe, NM 87501-2108
Products: Native art

* DISCOVER SANTA
FE INDIAN ARTS &
CRAFTS
PO Box 2847
Santa Fe, NM 87504-2847
Products: NA art

* EDITH LAMBERT
GALLERY
707 Canyon Dr
Santa Fe, NM 87501-2723
Products: NA art

* BOBBYS PLAZA
GALLERY
233 Canyon Rd
Santa Fe, NM 87501-2714
Products: NA art

BRUCE LAFOUNTAIN
Rt 19 Box 111V
Santa Fe, NM 87501
505-988-3703
Products: NA sculptor

FREE AIR FINE ART
PO Box 23285
Santa Fe, NM 87502
505-474-4480
Products: NA art

* HAND GRAPHICS
GALLERY
418 Montezuma Ave
Santa Fe, NM 87501-2579
Products: Indian handcrafts

* INSTITUTE OF
AMERICAN INDIAN
ARTS MUSEUM
PO Box 20007
Santa Fe, NM 87504-5007
505-988-6121
Products: NA art

JOAN CAWLEY
GALLERY
133 W San Francisco St
Santa Fe, NM 87501-2111
Products: NA art

* JOE WADE FINE
ARTS
102 E Water St
Santa Fe, NM 87501-2145
Products: Indian art, crafts

KIVA FINE ARTS
102 E Water St
Santa Fe, NM 87501
505-982-4273
Products: NA art, pottery, SW craftwork

MASLAK MCLEOD
607 Old Santa Fe Trail
Santa Fe, NM 87501
505-820-6389
Products: Inuit, Native,
Canadian

* NEW TRENDS
GALLERY
225 Canyon Rd
Santa Fe, NM 87501-2755
505-988-1199
Products: NA art, sculpture, crafts

* PACKARDS INDIAN
TRADING CO INC
61 Old Santa Fe Trail
Santa Fe, NM 87501-2009
800-648-7358
Products: NA pottery,
Indian items

PENA STUDIO
GALLERY
235 Don Gaspar
Santa Fe, NM 87501
505-820-1400
Products: NA posters,
T-shirts, art

* SCRIPSIT
3089 Plaza Blanca
Santa Fe, NM 87505-5341
505-471-1516
Info: Send SASE
Products: Paper and
leather calligraphy crafts

SPANISH AND INDIAN TRADING COMPANY, THE
924 Paseo de Peralta Ste 1
Santa Fe, NM 87501
505-983-6106
Products: Historic
American Indian

TSINNIES GALLERY
Box 537
Shiprock, NM 87420
505-368-5936
505-368-4240
Products: Navajo-made
jewelry; buckles, squash
blossoms, bracelets, ear-
rings, rings, conchos

* ED TALLER GALLERY
119 Bent St
Taos, NM 87571-5915
Products: NA art

BLUE RAIN GALLERY
115 Taos Plaza
Taos, NM 87571
505-751-0066
Products: NA art, NA
Kachinas and crafts.
Representing Pueblo
artists in arts and crafts

* LILLYS GALLERY
PO Box 342
Taos, NM 87571-0342
505-552-9501
Info: Send SASE
Products: Handcrafted
Acoma pottery and
figurines

NEW YORK

BLITZ ANTIQUE NATIVE AMERICAN ART LTD
PO Box 400
Crompond, NY 10517
914-739-9683
Products: Specializing in
NA articles of childhood

* ARCTIC ARTISTRY
2 Spring St
Hastings On Hudson
NY 10706-1511
914-478-7179
Brochure: Available of
sculpture
Products: All NA arts,
with special emphasis
on Inuit prints, sculp-
ture and tapestries, NA
jewelry, rugs

* M ZACHARY GALLERIES INC
347 Maple St
Hempstead
NY 11552-3252
Products: NA art, craft-
works

ADOBE ARTES
192 E Main St
Huntington, NY 11743
516-385-8410
Products: Trad/contemp
NA art, jewelry, pottery,
Kachinas, fetishes, bas-
kets

AMERICA HURRAH
766 Madison Ave
New York, NY 10021
212-535-1930
Products: Buyers/deal-
ers of pictorial bead-
work, Navajo weavings,
corn husk bags, NA
items

COMMON GROUND INC, THE
19 Greenwich Ave
New York, NY 10014
212-989-4178
Products: Antique and
contemporary arts of the
North American Indian

* AMERICAN INDIAN COMMUNITY HOUSE GALLERY
708 Broadway
New York, NY 10003
212-598-0100
Products: NA exhibits
and presentations of art

J CACCIOLA GALLERY
125 Wooster
New York, NY 10012
212-966-9177
Products: Contemporary
artwork from a variety
of artists, including Tony
and Elizabeth Abeyta

* New listings, NA = Native American,
SW = Southwest.

KOKOPELLI
New York, NY
603-569-4416
Products: Gallery featuring SW and NA jewelry; hand-crafted carvings and fetishes, more

TROTO-BONO
PO Box 34
Shrub Oak, NY 10588
914-528-6604
By appointment
Products: Indian and Eskimo artifacts of North America

TRADITIONS
Marty Gingras
7834 North Rd
Victor, NY 14564
716-924-7826
Products: Historic American Indian artifacts

NORTH CAROLINA

BIG MEAT POTTERY
Cherokee, NC 28719
704-497-9544
Products: Cherokee pottery

CHEROKEE HERITAGE MUSEUM AND GALLERY
Saunkook Village
Cherokee, NC 28719
704-497-3211
Products: Gift shop caries arts and crafts

* EL CAMINO INDIAN GALLERY
PO Box 482
Cherokee, NC 28719-0482
Products: NA art

OHIO

* AMERICAN INDIAN ARTS AND CRAFTS
352½ Erie
Cincinnati
OH 45208-1717
Products: NA art and crafts

OKLAHOMA

* BEAR ART GALLERY
RR 3 Box 1595
Afton, OK 74331-9016
Products: NA art

* CIRCLE TURTLE GALLERY
PO Box 986
Anadarko, OK 73005-0986
Products: NA art and merchandise

* NANCY JANET L SMITH STUDIO
1929 W Nashville
Broken Arrow, OK 74012-4827
918-251 -8952
Info: Send SASE
Products: Traditional and contemporary Cherokee watercolors, oils, and acrylic paintings

* BILL GLASS STUDIO
HC 64 Box 39,B
Locust Grove
OK 74352-9325
918-479-8884
Info: Send SASE
Products: Stoneware sculptures, carvings, pottery and bronzes

* CRYING WIND GALLERY AND FRAMES
400 N Indiana Ave
Oklahoma City
OK 73106-2802
405-235-9991
Info: Send SASE
Products: Seminole patchwork, dolls, watercolor artwork

* GUSTAFSON GALLERIES AT THE COLLONADE
9606 N May Ave
Oklahoma City
OK 73120-2714
Products: NA art

INDIAN TERRITORY GALLERY
18 Sherlyn Ln
Sapulpa, OK 74066-8826
Products: NA art

* KELLY HANEY ART GALLERY
PO Box 103
Seminole
OK 74818-0103
Products: NA art

**DEEK CREEK
GALLERY**
RR1 Box 120
Stillwater, OK 74074-9706
Products: NA art

* ART MARKET
7913 E 51st St
Tulsa, OK 74145-7841
Products: NA art

*** FRAMESMITH
GALLERY**
6528 E 101st St
Tulsa, OK 74133-6754
Products: NA art

OREGON

*** FRAME DESIGN &
SUNBIRD GALLERY**
916 NW Wall
Bend, OR 97701-2022
Products: NA art;
frames

*** SILVERSTAR
GALLERY**
PO Box 693
Carlton, OR 97111-0693
503-852-6644
Products: Paintings,
sculptures, jewelry,
Native owned

* ALDER GALLERY
55 West Broadway
Eugene, OR 97401
541-342-6411
Products: NA art and
crafts

*** ART OF THE
VINEYARD INC**
1430 Willamette St
Ste 24
Eugene, OR 97401-4049
Products: NA art

*** WIND SONG
GALLERY**
Seven Southeast Court
Pendleton, OR 97801
541-276-7993
Flyer/Newsletter: $1
Products: Handmade
NA dolls, paintings,
artifacts, pottery, knives
moccasins, dream catch-
ers, bows

* MERCIER FINE ART
1460 SW 66th
Portland, OR 97225
503-297-4158
Products: Graphite
drawings, paintings and
art, portraits, choice of
media and size in cus-
tom work

PLAID RABBIT, THE
111 NW 2nd Ave
Portland, OR 98209
503-224-0678
Products: "Purveyors of
fine art and political
memorabilia," some NA
art

PENNSYLVANIA

**FOUR WINDS
GALLERY**
5512 Walnut St
Shadyside Pittsburgh
PA 15232
412-682-5092
Products: NA pottery,
Kachinas, paintings,
sculpture, jewelry

SOUTH
CAROLINA

*** WOLF CREEK
GALLERY**
1315 Celebrity Cir
Myrtle Beach, SC 29577
803-448-4780
Products: Jewelry, fetishes, books, Music, prints,
sculpture, T-shirts, drums,
knives, kachinas, books

SOUTH
DAKOTA

*** FEATHERSTONE
PRODUCTIONS**
PO Box 487
Brookings, SD 57006-0487
605-693-3183
Info: Send SASE
Products: Sculptures
and original paintings

* New listings, NA = Native American,
SW = Southwest.

* T & K GALLERY OF NATIVE AMERICAN ARTISTS
430 Mt Rushmore Rd
Custer, SD 57730-1929
605-673-4121
Products: Bronzes, oils, watercolor and lithographs; handmade jewelry and beadwork

* CHEYENNE CROSSING GALLERY
HC 37 Box 1220
Lead, SD 57754-9716
Products: NA art and merchandise

* OSCAR HOWE ART CENTER
PO Box 1161
Mitchell, SD 57301-3410
605-996-4111
Price list/postcards: $675
Products: NA reproductions by Oscar Howe, Yanktonai Sioux T-shirts

* DAHL FINE ARTS CENTER
713 17th St
Rapid City, SD 57701-3613
Products: NA art

* GALLERY 306
310 S Phillips Ave
Sioux Falls
SD 57102-0719
Products: NA art

NORTHERN PLAINS GALLERY
American Indian Services
PO Box 1720
Sioux Falls, SD 57101
800-658-4797
Products: N Plains tribal arts visual and literary juried touring exhibitions; more

* TEKAKWITHA
PO Box 208
Sisseton, SD 57262-0208
Products: Native American art

* GALLERY 21
PO Box 550
Sturgis, SD 57785-0550
Products: NA art

TENNESSEE

TAFACHADY GALLERY OF ARTS AND GIFTS
101 Frazier Ave
Chattanooga, TN 37405
423-756-2797
Products: NA arts and crafts

* GARNMEISTER ART GALLERY
PO Box 686
Knoxville, TN 37901-0686
Products: NA art

TEXAS

GALLERY OF THE REPUBLIC
98 San Jacinto
Austin, TX 78767
512-472-7701
Products: NA art

* NATIVE AMERICAN IMAGES
PO Box 746
Austin, TX 78767-0746
800-252-3332
Catalog: Free
Products: Paintings, lithographs, prints, posters by Cherokee artist Donald Vann

* GALERIA SAN YSIDRO
PO Box 17913
El Paso, TX 79917-7913
Products: Native art, SW style furniture, home accessories

* CONTEMPORARY NATIVE AMERICAN ART
1028 Yale St
Houston, TX 77008-6922
Info: Send SASE
Products: Oil paintings, pen and ink drawings, pastels, airbrush, and portraits

*** BLUE GEM SHOP &
GALLERY**
311 Dodson St
Midland, TX 79701-6334
Products: Indian art,
jewelry

* ANNESLEY STUDIO
PO Box 3
Missouri City
TX 77459-0003
713-729-8960
Info: Free
Products: Bronze sculptures, drawings, paintings, pastels

*** WHITEWOLF
PHOTOGRAPHY**
PO Box 297
Redwater, TX 75573-0297
Info: Send SASE
Products: Original photographs with NA and
western themes

*** CHISHOLM TRAIL
GALLERY**
20 Chisholm Tr
Round Rock
TX 78681-5043
Products: NA art

*** GALLERY OF THE
SOUTHWEST**
13485 Blanco Rd
San Antonio,
TX 78216-2132
Products: NA art

*** GALERIA DE LAS
AMERICAS**
10189 Socorro Road
Socorro, TX 79927-2342
Products: Indian art,
handcrafts

*** PATHFINDERS
ARTWORKS**
260504 Preston
Spring, TX 77373-8337
Products: NA art

UTAH

**FULL SPIRIT
PUBLISHING**
PO Box 511515
Salt Lake City
UT 84151-1515
800-555-8313
Products: NA-theme
limited edition prints

VIRGINIA

BUFFALO GALLERY
127 S Fairfax St
Alexandria,
VA 22314-3301
Products: NA art

**PERRY HOUSE
GALLERIES**
Alexandria, VA
703-836-5148
Products: Paintings,
beadwork, portraits,
wearable art, bags, moccasins, gauntlets, more

* AMERIND GALLERY
PO Box 588
Daleville, VA 24083-0588
Products: NA art

**RETHA WALDEN
GAMBARO**
Sculptor
74 Dishpan Ln
Stafford, VA 22554
703-659-0130
Products: NA sculptor

WASHINGTON

LELOOSKA GALLERY
165 Merwin Village Rd
Ariel, WA 98603
306-225-9735
Products: NA jewelry
and art

*** ELEMENTS
GALLERY**
10500 NE 8th St
Bellevue, WA 98004-4351
Products: NA art

*** HOWARD
MANDEVILLE
GALLERY**
120 W Dayton St
Edmonds, WA 98020-4180
Products: NA art

ANCESTRAL SPIRITS GALLERY
921 Washington St
Port Townsend
WA 98368
360-385-0078
Products: Original drawings/art, limited edition prints, sculpture, baskets, carvings

*** TIN NA TIT KIN NE KI Indian Arts and Crafts**
PO Box 1057
Republic, WA 99166-1057
509-775-3077
Video/photos/info pkg: Available
Products: NA art from across North America Dating from 1813 to the present

*** ALASKA EAGLE ARTS**
PO Box 4518
Seattle, WA 98104-0518
Products: NA art and crafts

*** BAILEY NELSON GALLERY**
2001 Western Ave
Seattle, WA 98121-2163
Products: NA art

BRUCE BOYD CURIOSERI
Seattle, WA
206-328-7969
Products: Historic baskets, bead work, weaving, and wood/ivory carvings by NW Coast Eskimo folk

*** DAYBREAK STAR ARTS CENTER**
PO Box 99100
Seattle, WA 98199-0100
Products: NA art, crafts, merchandise, exhibits, events

*** FLURY & CO**
PO Box 4400
Seattle, WA 98104-0400
206-587-0260
Products: Vintage photography and antique NA art

*** MARIANNE PARTLOW GALLERY**
500 S Washington St
Seattle, WA 98104-2750
Products: Indian gallery art

*** STONINGTON GALLERY**
2030 First Ave
Seattle, WA 98121-2112
206-443-1108
Products: Represents work from all the tribes along the Northwest Coast, Traditional/Contemporary

*** CORONA COMPANY**
1150 Industry Drive
Tukwila, WA 98188-4803
Products: Native American art

WISCONSIN

*** BUFFALO ART CENTER**
PO Box 51
Bayfield, Wl 54814-0051
Products: NA art

WYOMING

JORDAN GALLERY
Cody, WY
800-531-4202
Products: Specializes in cowboy and American Indian memorabilia and used, rare books about West

*** CENTER STREET GALLERY**
PO Box 4059
Jackson, WY 83001-4059
Products: NA art

*** GALLERY OF THE WEST**
PO Box 4046
Jackson, WY 83001-4046
Products: NA art

CANADA

BANFFS NATURAL HISTORY MUSEUM
PO Box 1362
Banff, Alberta
Canada Y0L 0C0
Products: NA artifacts and collectibles

JAMES B MIGHTON
Antique Indian Art
Bay 5, 417-53rd Ave SE
Calgary, Alberta
Canada T2H 2E7
403-241-0732
Products: Antique Indian art and craftwork

HELMER ARTS
Golden, BC, Canada
604-344-5358
Products: Early North American Indian and Oceanic art

HELIN FINE ARTS GALLERY
Northwest Tsimshian Art
486 West Island Hwy
Parksville, BC
Canada V6P 1H2
800-894-3300
Info: Call or write
Products: Tsimshian gold and silver jewelry by Bill Helin

THUNDERBIRD GALLERY
3105-115 Fulford
Gangles Rd
Salt Spring Island, BC
Canada V8K 2T9
800-665-4433
Products: Northwest Native art and crafts, carvings

WILPS TSA-AK GALLERY
2426 Marine Dr West
Vancouver, BC
Canada V7V 1L1
604-925-5771
Products: Wood sculpture, gold and silver jewelry, limited edition prints

ALCHERINGA GALLERY
Victoria, BC, Canada
604-383-8224
Products: Ongoing contemporary tribal art from Canadian, NW coast aboriginal Australia and New Guinea

ART OF MAN GALLERY
Victoria, BC, Canada
604-383-3800
Products: NA and Eskimo exhibitions

ANCESTRAL JOURNEY GALLERY LTD
1141 Fort St
Victoria, BC
Canada V8V 3K9
604-380-2883
Products: "A spiritual journey in fine West Coast Native Art"

MASLAK MCLEOD
25 Prince Arthur Ave
Toronto, Ontario
Canada M5R 1B2
416-944-2577
Products: Inuit, Native, Canadian

HALLEGENIC ART
Woodstock, Ontario
Canada N4S 7V7
519-421-7350
Products: Canadian Inuit and Indian

JAPAN

GALLERY SEDONA
16-61 Kita 5 Chome
Higashikaigan, Chigasaki
Kanagawa 253 Japan
0467-87-0811
Products: Specialty store of NA arts, crafts in Japan, specially for Hopi silver crafts

---

* New listings, NA = Native American,
SW = Southwest.

Traditional Native American Arts and Crafts

ALABAMA

* SANDS OF TIME
1118 E Saunders Rd
Lot #1039
Dothan, AL 36301-6701
334-794-0894 after 3 pm
Catalog: $2
Products: Indian art
and dolls

ALASKA

*** ALASKA NATIVE
HOSPITAL
CRAFTS SHOP**
PO Box 7
Anchorage, AK 99501
Products: NA items

*** ALASKAN
TREASURES**
2900 Boniface Pky #134
Anchorage
AK 99504-3195
Products: Indian items

*** ANCHORAGE
MUSEUM SHOP**
121 W Seventh Ave
Anchorage
AK 99501-3611
907-343-4163
No catalog
Products: Alaska
Native crafts, ivory
carvings, soapstone,
beading, dolls, masks,
jewelry, books

*** BOREAL
TRADITIONS**
939 W 5th Ave Ste J
Anchorage
AK 99501-2032
Products: Alaskan
Native art and crafts

* INUA
Box 113224
Anchorage
AK 99511-3224
907-346-1055
Products: Handcarved
Alaskan ivory; Native
crafts and baskets

*** TAHETA ARTS AND
CULTURAL GROUP**
605 A St
Anchorage
AK 99501-3623
907-272-5829
Info: $1
Products: Carvings,
baskets, moccasins,
mukluks, jewelry, fans,
parkas, masks, art

*** ARCTIC ARTISANS
INC**
24562 Park Dr
Chugiak, AK 99567-6225
Products: NA art

*** ARCTIC TRAVELERS
GIFT SHOP**
201 Cushman St
Fairbanks
AK 99701-4639
907-456-7080
Brochure: Free
Products: Alaskan
Native arts, crafts, grass
baskets, ivory carvings,
eskimo figurines, books

*** ST LAWRENCE
ISLAND ORIGINAL
IVORY**
PO Box 189
Gambell, AK 99742-0189
Price list: Send SASE
Products: Bracelets,
cribbage boards, baleen
boats, etchings, ivory
carvings of animals

INUA
PO Box 4243
Homer, AK 99603
907-235-6644
Products: Handcarved
Alaskan ivory, Native
crafts and baskets

*** ALASKA STATE
MUSEUM SHOP**
395 Whittier St
Juneau, AK 99801-1718
907-465-2901
Products: NA art and
crafts

* New listings, NA = Native American,
SW = Southwest.

* AMOS WALLACE
PO Box 478
Juneau, AK 99802
907-586-9000
Info: Send SASE
Products: Carved silver
and gold jewelry; totem
poles, masks, and paddles

* MT JUNEAU
TRADING POST
151 S Franklin St
Juneau, AK 99801-1321
907-586-3426
Photos & prices:
Available
Products: Indian and
Eskimo arts and crafts;
ivory, soapstone, whale
bone, argilite carvings;
masks

* NANA MUSEUM OF
THE ARCTIC CRAFT
SHOP
PO Box 49
Kotzebue, AK 99752-0049
907-442-3304
Info: $1
Products: Dolls, masks,
baskets, carvings, jewel-
ry, ulus

* SAVOONGA NATIVE
STORE
PO Box 100
Savoonga
AK 99769-0100
Price list: Send SASE
Products: Figurines,
scrimshaw, ivory carv-
ings, jewelry

* NATIVE CARVINGS
& GIFTS
PO Box 226
Skagway, AK 99840
Products: Alaskan
Native items

* WANDAS CREATIVE
GIFTS
PO Box 314
Skagway, AK 99840
Products: Indian items

ARIZONA

* CHAMBERS
TRADING POST
PO Box 129
Chambers
AZ 86502-0129
Products: NA merchan-
dise

CIBECUE TRADING
COMPANY
31 N Cromwell Rd
Cibecue, AZ 85911
520-332-2575
Products: NA merchan-
dise

* EAST WEST ART
ANTIQUES CO, THE
PO Box 156
Cortaro, AZ 85652-0156
Products: Indian artifacts

* MUSEUM OF
NORTHERN
ARIZONA
Museum Shop/Bookstore
RR 4 Box 720
Flagstaff, AZ 86001-9302
800-423-1069
Products: NA merchan-
dise, and SW books

APACHE CULTURAL
CENTER
PO Box 700
Ft Apache, AZ 85926
520-338-4625
Products: NA art and
crafts

* CHEES INDIAN
STORE INC
PO Box 66 I-40 Exit 351
Houck, AZ 86506-0066
520-688-2603
Catalog: None
Products: Navajo rugs,
potteries, dolls, beaded
jewelry, drums, moc-
casins, curio items

* HOPI KIVA
PO Box 96
Kykotsmovi Village
AZ 86039-0096
Products: Hopi mer-
chandise

**MESA SOUTHWEST
MUSEUM**
City of Mesa Parks
53 N Macdonald St
Mesa, AZ 85201
602-644-2230
Products: NA art and
crafts; sponsors pow-
wows

* **INDIAN PONY
TRADING POST**
PO Box 413
Patagonia
AZ 85624-0413
Products: NA merchan-
dise

**MAZATZAL CASINO
GIFT SHOP**
PO Box 1820
Payson, AZ 85547
520-474-6044
Products: NA arts and
crafts

* **INDIAN RUINS
TRADING POST**
PO Box 46
Sanders, AZ 86512-0046
Products: NA art, crafts,
and merchandise

EASTERN COWBOYS
4235 N 86th Pl
Scottsdale
AZ 85251-2907
602-945-9804
Brochure: Free
Catalog: Available
Products: Sterling jew-
elry, rugs, baskets, pot-
tery, artifact recreations,
specialty items

* **FOUTZ INDIAN
ROOM**
7140 E 1st St
Scottsdale
AZ 85251-4306
Products: Navajo arts
and crafts

* **IVERSONS INDIAN
ARTS AND CRAFTS**
7120 E 6th Ave
Scottsdale
AZ 85251-3210
Products: NA arts and
crafts

* **WHITE HOGAN
SILVERMITHS**
7144 First Ave
Scottsdale
AZ 85251-4306
602-945-5556
Products: Distinctive
home and personal
accessories with lines of
traditional Navajo
motifs

HONANI CRAFTS
Hopi Cultural Center
PO Box 317
Second Mesa
AZ 86043-0317
602-734-2238 Info: Send
SASE
Products: Jewelry, pot-
tery, rugs, weavings,
baskets, Kachinas, art

**HOPI ARTS AND
CRAFTS SILVERCRAFT**
PO Box 37
Second Mesa, AZ 86043
520-734-2463
Products: Handcrafted
Hopi overlay jewelry;
Kachinas, baskets, pot-
teries, paintings, textiles

* **BEST LITTLE SHOP
IN SEDONA**
270 N Hwy 89-A
Sedona, AZ 86336-4237
Products: NA art and
craftwork

* **DINETHAH SILVER
GALLERY**
Ste B4 Hozho Hwy 179
Sedona, AZ 86336
Products: Navajo jewel-
ry

* **GIFTED HANDS
TLAQUEPAQUE**
PO Box 1388
Sedona, AZ 86339-1388
Products: NA hand-
crafts, other items

* New listings, NA = Native American,
SW = Southwest.

* MANY MOONS INDIAN SHOP
320 N 89 Hwy A
Sedona, AZ 86336-4243
Products: Indian artworks

MARGARET PATRICIO ARTS AND CRAFTS
PO Box 1381
Sells, AZ 85634
520-383-2800
Products: NA arts and crafts

* SAN JUAN SOUTHERN PAIUTE YINGUP WEAVERS
PO Box 1336
Tuba City
AZ 86045-1336
602-526-7143
Info: Call or write
Products: Paiute basketry

* ARIZONA SONORA DESERT MUSEUM GIFT SHOP
2021 N Kinney Rd
Tucson, AZ 85743-9719
Products: NA art and crafts

* ARTIFACTS
6212 E Brian Kent
Tucson, AZ 85710-1109
Products: Artifacts

* BLACK ARROW TRADERS
2400 N Calle de Maurer
Tucson, AZ 85749-9582
Products: NA merchandise

GREY DOG TRADING CO
2970 N Swan Rd Ste 138
Tucson, AZ 85712
520-881-6888
Products: Kachina dolls, pottery, textiles, jewelry, basketry, Zuni fetishes

* HATATHLI GALLERY Navajo Com College Dev
Navajo Rt 12 X Rt 64
Tsaile, AZ 86556
602-724-3311 ext 156
Call or write; no mail order
Products: Jewelry, art, rugs, sand paintings, beadwork

* BENALLYS INDIAN ARTS
PO Box 780
Window Rock, AZ
86515-0780
Products: Navajo art and crafts

NAVAJO ARTS AND CRAFTS ENTERPRISE
PO Box 160
Window Rock, AZ 85034
602-871-4090
Info: Send SASE
Products: Navajo arts and crafts, Apache burden baskets, earrings

ARKANSAS

* BILL & MARY HORN
RR 9 Box 227
Pine Bluff, AR 71603-9804
501-879-1066
Info: Call or write
Products: Jewelry, pottery, baskets and cornhusk dolls, beadwork, wooden necklaces

CALIFORNIA

* AMERICAN RIVER ANTIQUES & TRADING POST
180 Sacramento St
Auburn, CA 95603-5019
Products: NA art and crafts

* TATEWIN-PETAKI AMERICAN INDIAN ARTS & CRAFTS
PO Box 549
Big Bear City
CA 92314-0549
714-585-1435
Info: Call or write
Products: Beadwork, tapestries, dolls, hairpipe chokers, leatherwork

29

* **BEAR MOUNTAIN TRADING CO**
PO Box 6503
Big Bear Lake
CA 92315-6503
Products: NA merchandise

* **EASTERN SIERRA TRADING CO**
PO Box 731
Bridgeport
CA 93517-0731
619-932-7231
No mail order
Products: Turquoise and silver jewelry, beadwork, pottery, and baskets

* **BUNTE & SHAW TRADING CO**
651 Citadel Ave
Claremont, CA 91711-5523
Products: NA merchandise

* **PNACI INTERTRIBAL EMPORIUM**
PO Box 2377
Diamond Springs
CA 95619
916-676-2240
Catalog: $5
Products: Fine art, collectibles, miniature warbonnets, weapons, bronzes, paintings, crafts

* **CRAFT AND FOLK CRAFTS MUSEUM AND GIFTS**
5800 Wilshire Blvd
Los Angeles
CA 90036-4501
Products: NA art and crafts

* **OPHELIA JOHNSONS INDIAN VARIETY SHOP**
10256 Central Ave
Montclair
CA 91763-3802
714-445-8451
Info: Send SASE
Products: Baskets, silver and shell jewelry, beadwork, pottery, dolls

* **INTERTRIBAL TRADING POST**
523 E 14th St
Oakland, CA 94606-2909
Products: NA art, crafts, and merchandise

* **PAINTED DESERT**
PO Box 201
Salinas, CA 93902-0201
408-757-2536
Products: NA merchandise

* **APACHE INDIAN ARTS CENTER**
2425 San Diego Ave
San Diego
CA 92110-2876
Products: NA crafts

* **APACHE TRADING POST**
2801 Juan St
San Diego
CA 92110-2714
Products: NA art and crafts

* **ENBEE COLLECTIBLES**
6435 Crystalaire Dr
San Diego, CA 92120-3833
Products: NA items

* **LOVE FLUTES**
PO Box 9307
San Diego
CA 92169-0307
800-4-FLUTES
Brochure: Free
Products: NA cedar flutes

* **INDIAN ART CENTER OF CALIFORNIA**
12666 Ventura Blvd
Studio City
CA 91604-2414
818-763-3430
No catalog
Products: Established 1966, An inventory of 10,000 items from 60 Native tribes

* **YPPARAGUIRRE TRADING POST**
711 South Mathilda Ave
Sunnyvale
CA 94087-1309
Products: NA items

* New listings, NA = Native American, SW = Southwest.

EAGLES PEAK TRADING POST
11708 Millard Canyon Rd
Banning, CA 92220
Products: NA crafts, books

* CHIEF GEORGE PIERRE TRADING POST
PO Box 3202
Torrance, CA 90510-3202
213-372-1048
Info: Send SASE
Products: Rugs, silver/turquoise jewelry, Kachinas, beadwork

* GOING TO THE SUN STUDIO
1063 Hillendale Ct
Walnut Creek
CA 94596-6214
415-939-8803
Info: Call or write,
Products: Art, sculpture, tapestries, Fabric, painted skins, parfleches, drums, beadwork, shawls

* BADGERPAW INDIAN CRAFTS
PO Box 2016
Weaverville, CA 96093
916-423-6336
No Catalog,
Products: Traditional & contemporary NA arts, crafts, Collectible baskets and pottery

COLORADO

* NOWETAHS INDIAN STORE AND MUSEUM
Rt 27 Box 40
New Portland
ME 04954-9602
207-628-4981
Free brochure: Lists 12 catalogs
Products: 12 separate catalogs for NA crafts, gifts, drums, jewelry, dolls, clothing, pottery, more

CHARLES EAGLE PLUME STORES INC
PO Box 447
Allenspark
CO 80510-0447
303-747-2861
Products: Arts and crafts of the NA and houses the Charles Eagle Plume Collection of art

* ARIZONA ROOM
7635 Downywood Ct
Colorado Springs
CO 80920-6618
Products: NA merchandise

* EAGLE DANCER TRADING CO
Cooper Creek Square #223
Winter Park
CO 80482-9999
Products: NA merchandise

* DON WOODWARDS INDIAN TRADING POST
27688 Hwy 160
Cortez, CO 81321-9366
Products: NA merchandise

* COLORADO WEST
Stapleton International Airport
Denver, CO 80207
Products: NA merchandise

* D & H GIFTS
1281 Phillips Dr
Denver, CO 80233-1259
Products: NA crafts

* DIAMOND CIRCLE INDIAN GIFT SHOP
651 Main Ave
Durango
CO 81301-5423
Products: NA art, crafts, merchandise

* RICHS INDIAN ARTS
800 S Camino Del Rio
Ste 27
Durango, CO 71301-6889
Products: Indian items

* BENZAV TRADING CO
PO Box 911
Fort Collins
CO 80522-0911
Products: NA merchandise

PATRICIA ANN OF COLORADO
PO Box 291
Idledale, CO 80453
303-674-8863
Products: NA arts and crafts

* DEER TRACK TRADERS LTD
Box 448
Loveland
CO 80539-0448
970-669-6750
Wholesale only
Products: Navajo, Zuni jewelry, sandpaintings, rugs, dolls, beadwork, cards, prints, crafts

CONNECTICUT

* ALEXANDER KOZLOV
153 Priscilla St
Bridgeport, CT 06610
203-374-5214
Products: Of Russian extract, he produces beautiful replicated art of Plains Indians; beadwork, more

DISTRICT OF COLUMBIA

* INDIAN CRAFT SHOP, THE
Dept of the Interior
1849 C St NW
Washington, DC 20240
202-208-4056
Products: Jewelry, pottery, sand paintings, kachinas, Alaskan ivory, basketry, fetishes

* NAICA COLLECTIBLES
5332 Wisconsin Ave NW
Ste 138
Washington DC
20015-2001
202-561-1354
Info: Write or call
Products: Jewelry, carvings, pottery, beadwork

FLORIDA

* THIS N THAT
204 Brevard Ave
Cocoa Village
FL 32922-7907
407-631-6609
Products: Old pawn and contemporary jewelry, moccasins, books and kachinas, fetishes, pottery

* MICCOSUKEE GIFT SHOP & CULTURAL CENTER
Tamiami Station
PO Box 440021
Miami, FL 33144
Products: Miccosukee craftworks

JOLIMA INDIAN CRAFTS
1403 N 57th Ave
Pensacola
FL 32506-4007
Products: NA merchandise

IDAHO

* EAGLE SPRINGS GIFT SHOP
Kootenai River Plaza
Bonners Ferry, ID 83805
Products: NA merchandise

* KAMIAKIN KRAFTS
PO Box 358
Fort Hall, ID 83203-0358
208-785-2546
Price list: Send SASE
Products: Beadwork belts, buckles and watch bands, earrings, coin purses, necklaces, moccasins

---

* New listings, NA = Native American,
SW = Southwest.

WARPATH TRADING POST
Coeur D'Alene Nation
PO Box 609
Plummer, ID 83851
208-686-5501
Products: NA designed jewelry and clothing, Pendleton blankets, pottery, regalia, replica pieces

ILLINOIS

* CROW-FROG CRAFTS
24255 South 1th Ave
Broadview, IL 60153
Catalog available
Products: Traditional arts and crafts
Beadwork, chokers, breastplates Craft making supplies

* SOUTHWEST EXPRESSIONS
900 N Michigan Ave
Ste 600
Chicago, IL 60611-1542
Products: NA and SW-inspired items

* BEAR PAW INC
217 N Ferry St Apt A
Rockton, IL 61072-2628
Products: NA items

INDIANA

* SOUTHWEST OUTPOST
5302 Madison Ave
Indianapolis
IN 46227-4244
317-783-3854
Catalog: Free
Products: SW accessories, home decor, gifts
Authentic NA items, dolls, moccasins, art, books

KANSAS

PHANTOM ART
Rt 3 Box 450
Harlan, KS 66967
913-346-5929
Products: Handpainted buffalo skulls

* INDIAN MUSEUM GIFT SHOP
650 N Seneca St
Wichita, KS 67203-3204
Products: NA art, crafts, and merchandise

KENTUCKY

* FOUR FEATHERS INDIAN ARTS
627 Main St
Covington
KY 41011-1331
Products: NA arts, crafts, and merchandise

* MYSTIC OWL TRADING POST
733 Cheryl Ln
Lexington, KY 40504-3607
606-277-2475
List with photos: $2
Products: Reproduction NA beadwork, quillwork, war clubs, shields, spears, bows, arrows, knives

LOUISIANA

* NATIVE AMERICAN ARTS OF THE SOUTH
PO Box 217
Elton, LA 70532-0217
318-584-5130
Price list: Send SASE
Products: Pottery, swamp cane, white oak, and long-leaf pine needle baskets

MAINE

* NOWETAHS INDIAN STORE AND MUSEUM
Rt 27 Box 40
New Portland
ME 04954-9602
207-628-4981
Free brochure: Lists 12 catalogs
Products: 12 separate catalogs for NA crafts, gifts, drums, jewelry, dolls, clothing, pottery, more

* WABANAKI ARTS
PO Box 453
Old Town
ME 04468-0453
207-827-3447
Price list: Send SASE
Products: Penobscot
carved canes & war
clubs, totem poles, stone
tomahawks, baskets,
beadwork

* LONGACRE ENTERPRISES
PO Box 196
Perry, ME 04667
207-853-2762
Price list: Send SASE
Products: Bow / arrow
racks, incense burners,
driftwood lamps,
Passamaquoddy birch
bark

* BASKET BANK Aroostook Micmac Council
8 Church St
Presque Isle
ME 04769-2410
207-853-2762
Price list: Send SASE
Products: Potato, pack,
clothes, fishing, decora-
tive, shopping, cradle,
and sewing baskets

MARYLAND

* INDIAN RIVER TRADING CO
11441 Coastal Hwy
Ocean City
MD 21842-2516
Products: NA merchan-
dise

NATIVE SPIRIT
12512 Arbor View Terr
Silver Spring, MD 20902
303-946-9338
Brochure: $1
Products: Buckskin
medicine bags and ster-
ling silver jewelry,
dream catchers, over 50
different items

MASSACHUSETTS

* SILVER STAR Wampanoa Crafts
PO Box 402
Middleboro
MA 02346-0402
617-947-4159
Info: Send SASE
Products: Moccasins,
beadwork, leather
crafts, baskets, quill-
work, wall plaques

SUN BASKET
8½ Bearskin Neck
Rockport MA 01966-1664
508-546-7546
Brochure: Free
Products: Jewelry,
Pueblo pottery,
kachinas, sandpaintings,
Zuni fetishes, carvings,
baskets, more

* AMERICAN INDIAN STORE
139 Walter St
Roslindale,
MA 02131-1540
Products: NA arts & crafts

MICHIGAN

* SOUTHWEST MIRAGE
17268 Tremlett Dr
Clinton Township
MI 48035-2386
Products: SW-inspired
items

* MONADNOCK GIFT SHOP
PO Box 400
Macinaw City
MI 49701-9999
616-436-5131
No catalog
Products: Jewelry,
sandpaintings, pottery,
weavings, baskets,
fetishes, carvings, arts,
crafts

* New listings, NA = Native American,
SW = Southwest.

* MOON BEAR POTTERY
6135 E Broadway #7
Mount Pleasant
Ml 48858-8942
517-773-2510
Brochure: Send SASE
Products: Pottery, wall hangings, sculptures, oil paintings and drawings; dolls

* INDIAN HILLS TRADING CO & INDIAN ART
1681 Harbor Rd
Petosky, Ml 49770-9343
Info: Send SASE
Products: Quillwork, beadwork, drums, moccasins, Navajo rugs, SW silver/turquoise jewelry

* NATIVE WEST
863 West Ann Arbor Tr
Plymouth, Ml 48170-1601
313-455-8838
Products: Prints, posters, books, music, headdresses, dolls, drums, tomahawks, fetishes, jewelry, rugs

MINNESOTA

* LADY SLIPPER DESIGNS
RR 3 Box 556
Bemidji, MN 56601-9409
800-950-5903
Info: Send SASE
Products: Beaded charms, birch bark birdhouses, moccasins, baskets

* CHIPPEWA INDIAN CRAFT & GIFT SHOP
Red Lake Indian Reservation
Goodridge, MN 56725
Products: NA art and merchandise

* IKWE MARKETING
White Earth Reservation
Rt 1
Osage, MN 56570-9801
218-573-3411
Brochure: Send SASE
Products: Birch bark baskets, Ojibway beadwork, star quilts, braided rugs, quillwork

MISSISSIPPI

* CHOCTAW MUSEUM GIFT SHOP
PO Box 6010
Philadelphia
MS 39350-8821
601-650-1685
Price list: Free
Products: Choctaw-made crafts, from cane, beads, cloth, Books, T-shirts

MISSOURI

* SKYPAINTER
Kevin Turner
De Soto, MO 63020-5147
314-337-4105
Brochure/video: $5
Products: NA jewelry, wall hangings, paintings, painted skulls, artwork

MONTANA

* BLACKFEET CRAFTS ASSOCIATION
PO Box 51
Browning
MT 59417-0051
Products: NA merchandise

* BLACKFEET TRADING POST
PO Box 626
Browning
MT 59417-0626
406-338-2050
Info: Send SASE
Products: Moccasins, beadwork, baskets, pottery, shawls, and paintings

* SPIRIT TALK
Box 430
Browning, MT 59417
406-338-2882
Catalog: Send SASE
Products: Books, tapes, quillwork, buckskin, imitation eagle feathers, dance outfits, more

* CUSTER BATTLEFIELD TRADING POST
PO Box 246
Crow Agency
MT 59022-0246
Products: NA art, crafts, and merchandise

* CHARGING BEAR TRADING POST
PO Box 276
Ennis, MT 59729-0276
Products: NA merchandise

* TIPI GIFT SHOP, THE
HC 62 Box 3110E
Livingston, MT 59047-9621
406-222-8575
Info: Send SASE
Products: Paintings, sketches, knives, shields, star quilts

* COUP MARKS
PO Box 532
Ronan, MT 59864-0532
406-246-3216
Info: Send SASE
Products: Paintings, sculpture, ribbon shirts, moccasins, bead work, dolls, shawls, games

DOUG ALLARD'S TRADING POST
PO Box 460
St Ignatius, MT 59865
800-821 -3318
Catalog/brochure: Free
Products: Beadwork, jewelry, Pendleton blankets, beads, crafts, supplies, books, herbs, jams

K & M CREATIONS
PO Box 521
St Ignatius, MT 59865
406-745-4186
Color flyer: $3
Products: Beaded neck pouches, amulets, knifecases, strike-a-lites, strips, rosettes. Custom orders

NEBRASKA

* WICAHPI VISION
PO Box 859
Chadron, NE 69337-0859
Products: Indian items

* PILCHERS INDIAN STORE
Rt 2 Box 348 A
Fort Calhoun, NE 68023
402-468-5131
Info: Send SASE,
Products: Beadwork, roaches, bustles, pottery, Kachinas, Navajo silver jewelry

* FORT CODY TRADING POST
Interstate 80
North Platte, NE 69101
Products: NA merchandise

NEVADA

* LEHMAN CAVES GIFTS
Great Basin Nat'l Park
Baker, NV 89311
Products: NA art, crafts, and merchandise

* FALLON INDIAN TRADING POST
1017 Shoshone Dr
Fallon, NV 89406-9406
Products: NA merchandise

* FORT MCDERMITT PAIUTE SHOSHONE TRIBES
PO Box 457
Mc Dermitt
NV 89421-0457
Products: NA craftspersons may be located by contacting the Tribe

* CROSBY LODGE GIFT SHOP
Sutcliffe Star Rt
Reno, NV 89510
Products: NA merchandise

* EARTH WINDOW
Tahoe Visitors Ctr
135 N Sierra St
Reno, NV 89501-1304
Products: NA merchandise

* WINTER MOON
TRADING CO
PO Box 189
Schurz, NV 89427-0189
702-773-2510
Info: Send SASE,
Products: Beaded and
silver jewelry, horsehair
baskets, pottery and
original artwork

NEW JERSEY

* LONE BEAR INDIAN
CRAFT CO
300 Main St #F
Orange, NJ 07050-3628
Price list: Send SASE
Products: Woodland
beadwork, costumes,
war bonnets, head
dresses, collectibles

NEW MEXICO

* AGAPE
SOUTHWEST
POTTERY
414 Romero Rd NW
Albuquerque
NM 87104-1422
505-243-2366
Fax: 505-243-3002
Products: Traditional
handmade NA pottery,
jewelry, rugs, kachinas,
and paintings

* ARMADILLO
TRADING CO
201 Wellesley Dr SE
Albuquerque
NM 87106-1419
Products: NA merchan-
dise

* BALD EAGLE
TRADING POST
2921 Cutler Ave NE
Albuquerque
NM 87106-1714
Products: NA merchan-
dise

* BEAR PAW INDIAN
ARTS
326 Felipe NW
Old Town,
Albuquerque, NM 87104
Products: NA merchan-
dise

* BING CROSBYS
INDIAN ARTS
2510 Washington NE
Albuquerque
NM 87110-3913
505-888-4800
Products: Indian arts,
jewelry, pottery,
Kachinas, fetishes

* CIBOLA TRAIL
TRADERS EAST
PO Box 3362
Albuquerque
NM 87190-3362
Products: NA merchan-
dise

* ED YOUNGS, INC
2323 Krogh Ct NW
Albuquerque, NM 87104
505-764-9530
Catalog: Free
Products: Navajo, Zuni,
Hopi jewelry, Navaho
kachina dolls, animal
fetish necklaces, pottery

* INDIAN PUEBLO
CULTURAL CTR INC
2401 12th St NW
Albuquerque, NM
87104-2302
505-843-7270
Brochure/calendar of
events: Free
Products: Video, $7.95.
Pottery, kachinas, paint-
ings, jewelry, beadwork,
baskets, rugs, books,
more

RON MARTINEZ
330 Tribal Rd #65
Albuquerque, NM 87105
505-869-9303
Products: Isleta/Taos
Pueblo potter and artist;
teacher

* SQUASH BLOSSOM
322 N White Sands Blvd
Almagordo
NM 88310-7062
505-437-8126
Products: Navajo, Zuni
jewelry, and kachinas,
rugs, sand paintings,
baskets, sculptures

* CARLSBAD CAVERNS NAT'L PARK
PO Box Y
Carlsbad
NM 88221-7518
Products: NA merchandise

* BIG SKY TRADERS
PO Box 461
Corrales
NM 87048-0461
Products: NA merchandise

* JICARILLA ARTS & CRAFTS SHOP
PO Box 507
Dulce, NM 87528-0507
Brochure: Free
Products: Beadwork, baskets, leatherwork, paintings

ROBERT DALE TSOSIE
Rt 1 Box 204-A
Espanola, NM 87532
505-747-1657/505-699-5662
Products: NA artisan, sculptor

* CORN STUDIO
PO Box 1420
Espanola
NM 87532-1420
Products: NA art and crafts

ARROYO TRADING COMPANY
2111 West Apache
Farmington, NM 87401
505-326-7427
505-327-3711
Products: Sand paintings, clocks, lamps, pottery, frames, custom matting, UPS shipping

* FIFTH GENERATION TRADING CO
2838 W Main St
Farmington
NM 87401-3750
Products: NA merchandise

* RUSSELL FOUTZ INDIAN ROOM
301 W Main St
Farmington
NM 87401-8422
Products: NA arts and crafts

* HATCH BROTHERS TRADING POST
PO Box 8
Fruitland
NM 87416-0008
Products: NA items

* ANDYS TRADING POST
612 W Wilson Ave
Gallup, NM 87301-5328
Products: NA items

* APACHE TRADING CO
206 W Hwy 66
Gallup, NM 87301-6354
Products: NA merchandise

* ATKINSON TRADING CO
PO Box 566
Gallup, NM 87305-0566
Products: NA merchandise

* FIRST AMERICAN TRADERS
2201 W 66th St
Gallup, NM 87301
Products: NA merchandise

* INDIAN DEN TRADING CO
1111 Ceasaer
Gallup, NM 87301-4974
Products: NA merchandise

* INDIAN VILLAGE
2209 W Hwy 66
Gallup, NM 87301-6809
505-722-5524
Products: Zuni and Navajo jewelry, sand paintings, carvings, paintings, Kachinas

JOHNNY MURPHYS TRADING CO
1206 E 66th
Gallup, NM 87301
Products: NA merchandise

* New listings, NA = Native American, SW = Southwest.

* CAROL G LUCERO
PO Box 319
Jemez Pueblo
NM 87024-0319
505-843-9337
Info: Send SASE
Products: Pueblo pottery, baskets cedar
flutes, Kachinas, drums,
sculptures, Navajo dolls

*** ASHCROFT
TRADERS INC**
PO Box 1005
Kirtland
NM 87417-1005
Products: NA merchandise

*** CORN MAIDEN
GALLERY AND SHOP**
306 Calle de Guadalupe
Mesilla, NM 88046-9999
Products: NA art and
merchandise

*** LA TIENDA GIFT
SHOP**
Calle de Parian
Mesilla, NM 88046-9999
Products: NA merchandise

*** WINDMILL
TRADING COMPANY**
RR 22 Box 1297
Pena Blanca
NM 87041-1297
505-465-2416
Products: Specializing
in Santo Domingo
Indian crafts; jeweler's
supplies, wholesale/retail

*** ALTAS TRADING
POST**
PO Box 508
Roswell, NM 88202-0508
Products: NA craftwork

* PUEBLO POTTERY
PO Box 366
San Fidel,
NM 87049-0366
800-933-5771
Products: Pottery,
Kachinas, jewelry, fetishes, rugs, Acoma photographs, prints, art

*** OKE OWEENGE
ARTS & CRAFTS**
PO Box 1095
San Juan Pueblo
NM 87566-1095
505-852-2372
Price list: Send SASE
Products: Wall hangings, pillows, pottery,
dolls, beadwork, silver
jewelry, baskets, paintings. dolls, more

*** ANASAZI INDIAN
ARTS**
PO Box 319
Santa Cruz
NM 87567-0319
Products: NA items

**ANDREA FISHER
FINE POTTERY**
221 W San Francisco St
Santa Fe, NM 97501
505-986-1234
Products: Specializing
in the pottery of Maria
Martinez

*** CASA HOPI DE
SANTA FE**
114 Old Santa Fe Trail
Santa Fe, NM 87501-2105
Products: Hopi crafts

**CASE TRADING
POST MUSEUM SHOP**
704 Camino Lejo
Santa Fe, NM 87505
505-982-4636
Products: Unique
Indian arts and crafts

**CRAIG DAN
GOSEYUN STUDIO**
Rt 2 Box 305 A
Santa Fe, NM 87505
505-471-9218
Products: NA bronze
sculptor

JOHN GONZALES
Rt 5 Box 316
Santa Fe, NM 87501
505-455-2476/505-455-3432
Products: San Ildefonso
potter

* TED MILLER
CUSTOM KNIVES
PO Box 6328
Santa Fe
NM 87502-6328
505-984-0338
Price list: Send SASE
Products: Wood and
horn carvings, deer
horn pipes, elk horn belt
buckles, bolos, knives

WENDY PONCA
Ponca Designs
453 Cerrillos Rd
Santa Fe, NM 87501
505-989-1948
By appointment only
Products: NA jewelry
and crafts, beadwork

* WIND RIVER
TRADING CO
113 E San Francisco St
Santa Fe
NM 87501-2109
Products: Native
American art and crafts

* FOUTZ TRADING
CO
PO Box 1894
Shiprock
NM 87420-1894
505-368-5790
Products: Navajo arts
and crafts

* BROKEN ARROW
INDIAN ARTS &
CRAFTS
PO Box 1601
Taos, NM 87571-1601
Products: NA merchandise

* CARLS INDIAN
TRADING POST
PO Box 813
Taos, NM 87571-0813
Products: NA merchandise

SOUTHWEST
MOCCASIN AND
DRUM
PO Box 4904
Taos, NM 87571
505-758-9332
Products: Handmade
drums, and moccasins

STETSON
HONYUMPTEWA
c/o Blue Rain Gallery
115 McCarthy Plaza
Taos, NM 87571
800-414-4893
Products: Artisan in
creating Katsina dolls

* DURANS POTTERY
PO Box 339
Tesuque, NM 87574-
0339
Products: NA pottery

* CONTINENTAL
DIVIDE INDIAN
HANDCRAFTS
PO Box 1059
Thoreau
NM 87323-1059
Products: Indian handcrafts

* JEM TRADING POST
PO Box 395
Vanderwagen
NM 87326-0395
Products: NA items

* CIRCLE W PAWN &
TRADING CO
PO Box 256
Waterflow
NM 87421-0256
Products: NA merchandise

* HOGBACK
TRADING CO
Star Route Box 57
Waterflow, NM 87421
Products: Indian items

* PUEBLO OF ZUNI
ARTS & CRAFTS
PO Box 245
Zuni, NM 87327-0425
505-782-4481
Info: Send SASE
Products: Pottery,
fetishes, contemporary
art, Zuni turquoise,
shell, coral, jet, silver
jewelry

* New listings, NA = Native American,
SW = Southwest.

* BLUE JAYS POTTERY INC
PO Box 717
Zuni, NM 87327-0717
Products: NA pottery

NEW YORK

* BROOKLYN MUSEUM SHOP
200 E Pkwy
Brooklyn, NY 11238
Products: NA merchandise and art

* KIVA TRADING CO
117 Main St
Cold Spring Harbor
NY 11724-1403
Products: NA merchandise

* BLACK BEAR TRADING POST
PO Box 47
Esopus, NY 12429-0047
914-384-6786
Info: Send SASE
Products: Baskets, pottery, bead work, Kachinas, war clubs, soap stone and woodcarvings, more

IROQUOIS BONE CARVINGS
3560 Stony Pt Rd
Grand Island
NY 14072-1127
Products: Carved bone art

* AKWESASNE CULTURAL CENTER
Akwesasne Museum
Rt 37 RR 1 Box 14 C
Hogansburg
NY 13655-9705
518-358-2649
Price list: Send SASE
Products: Mohawk black ash splint and sweetgrass basketry

* MOHAWK IMPRESSIONS
PO Box 20
Hogansburg
NY 13655-0020
518-358-2467
Info: Send SASE
Products: Dolls, beadwork, baskets, Mohawk paintings, & other crafts

* CAYUGA TRADING POST
PO Box 523
Ithaca, NY 14851-0523
Products: NA merchandise

* AMERICAN INDIAN CRAFTS
719 Broad
Salamanca, NY 14779-1330
Products: NA art and crafts

* CHRIS JOHN FAMILY ARTS AND CRAFTS
RR2 Box 315
Red Hook
NY 12571-9529
Products: NA crafts

* SENECA IROQUOIS NAT'L MUSEUM GIFT SHOP
PO Box 422
Salamanca
NY 14779-0422
716-945-1738
Price list: Send SASE
Products: Books, cards, Iroquois, beadwork, silverwork, baskets, baskets, masks, dolls, rattles, jewelry, leathercraftscassette/video tapes, T-shirt, pottery

NORTH CAROLINA

BETTY MANEY
PO Box 170
Cherokee, NC 28719
704-497-7708
Products: Makes traditional Cherokee crafts, baskets, effigy pots jewelry, dolls, beaded items

* QUALLA ARTS & CRAFTS MUTUAL INC
PO Box 310
Cherokee
NC 28719-0310
704-497-3103
Products: Handmade crafts by Eastern Band Cherokee artisans; figurines, beadwork, pottery, etc

WOLF CREEK TRADERS
614 E Arlington Blvd
Greenville, NC 27858
Products: NA items

* WAYAH STI INDIAN TRADITIONS
PO Box 130
Hollister, NC 27844-0130
919-586-2546
Price list: Send SASE
Products: Beadwork,
leatherwork, stone
pipes, sculptures, pottery

* LUMBEE INDIAN ARTS & CRAFTS
Hope Sheppard
PO Box 1298
Pembroke
NC 28372-1298
910-521-9494
Info: Send SASE
Products: Baskets,
beadwork, leatherwork

OHIO

TRAIL OF DREAMS
110 Edwards Ave NW
Warren, OH 44483-1118
216-847-8853
No catalog
Products: Pottery, art,
prints, jewelry, dream-
catchers, mandalas
lamps, rugs, herbs,
kachinas

OKLAHOMA

* DIXON PALMER HEADDRESSES & TIPIS
RR 3 Box 189
Anadarko, OK 73005-9559
Products: NA head-
dresses and tipis

* OKLAHOMA INDIAN ARTS AND CRAFTS COOPERATIVE
PO Box 966
Anadarko
OK 73005-0966
405-247-3486
Price list: Send SASE
Products: Beaded moc-
casins, belts, ties, pins,
costumes, hand bags,
jewelry, shirts,

* ARROWOOD TRADING POST
2700 N Hwy 66
Catoosa, OK 74015-2317
Products: NA art and
crafts

* CHEROKEE TRADING POST
Interstate 40 at Custer
exit
Clinton, OK 73601
Products: NA merchan-
dise

* TOUCHING LEAVES INDIAN CRAFTS
927 Portland Ave
Dewey, OK 74029-1823
918-534-2859
Catalog: $1
Products: German sil-
ver jewelry and leather
crafts

* NATIVE TREASURES
313 E Third
Elk City, OK 73644
405-225-4208
Products: NA items

* AMERICAN INDIAN HANDCRAFTS
PO Box 533
Meeker, OK 74855-0533
405-279-3343
Brochure: Send SASE
Products: Ribbonwork
blankets, shirts, shawls,
beadwork and Feather
crafts

* CHOCTAW TRADING POST
1520 N Portland Ave
Oklahoma City
OK 73107-1524
Products: NA merchan-
dise

PAUL HACKER KNIVES AND FLUTES
6513 & 6505 NW 20th Dr
Oklahoma City
OK 73008
405-787-8600/405-789-2300
Products: Knives and
flutes made by member
of Choctaw Tribe

* New listings, NA = Native American,
SW = Southwest.

**CLIFTONS OSAGE
PRAIRIE GIFTS**
118 E Main
Pawhuska, OK 74056
918-287-3737
Products: Indian items

* ADAMS STUDIOS
RR 3 Box 615 A
Ponca City
OK 74604-8940
405-765-5086
Price list: Send SASE
Products: : Artwork,
beadwork, jewelry, rings

**MISTER INDIANS
COWBOY STORE**
1000 South Main St
Sapulpa, OK 74066-5448
918-224-6511
Price list: Free
Products: Rugs, pottery,
turquoise and silver, kachinas, moccasins, fans, gourds,
drums, art, supplies

**CHEROHAWK
TRADING CO**
430 S Muskogee Ave
Tahlequah, OK 74464
918-456-7195
Products: NA items

*** CHEROKEE ARTS &
CRAFTS CENTER**
PO Box 948
Tahlequah
OK 74465-0948
Products: NA art and
crafts

**CHEROKEE NAT'L
MUSEUM GIFT SHOP**
PO Box 515
Tahlequah
OK 74465-0515
Products: NA art and
crafts

* TAH MELS
PO Box 1123
Tahlequah
OK 74465-1123
918-456-5461
Info: Send SASE
Products: Dolls, beadwork, baskets, quilts,
jewelry, artwork, woodcarvings

OREGON

*** BURNS PAIUTE
TRIBE**
HC71 Box 100
Burns, OR 97720-9803
Products: Native
American hand crafts

*** CRATER LAKE
LODGE INC**
Crater Lake, OR 97604
Products: NA merchandise

* ARROWWOOD
30075 LaBleu Rd
Eugene, OR 97405-9437
541-342-7487
Products: NW NA arts
and crafts, traditional
and contemporary

**SOUTHWEST
JOURNEY**
296 E 5th St
Eugene, OR 97401
541-484-6804
Products: NA jewelry,
art, gourds, cards, gifts

*** HUICHOL INDIAN
ART**
Bonnie and Barry Joyce
HC 84 Box OL94
Myrtle Point, OR 97458
541-396-3289
Products: Indian art
from the Sierra Madres
of West Central Mexico

*** CONFEDERATED
TRIBES**
of the Umatilla Indians
PO Box 638
Pendleton
OR 97801-0638
Products: NA craftspersons may be located by
contacting the Tribe

*** DESIGNS OF
DESCENDING
TRADITIONS**
5931 SE Holgate Blvd
Portland, OR 97206-3831
503-777-2558
Products: Mirror/wood
cuts, beaded earrings,
dream catchers, canvas
teepees, wood designs

43

* CONFEDERATED TRIBES
of the Warm Springs
PO Box C
Warm Springs
OR 97761-3001
Products: Native American crafts persons may be contacted through the Tribe

IDA PATERSON
PO Box 282
Willamina, OR 97396
541-876-9642
Products: Grand Ronde Indian beadwork

PENNSYLVANIA

* EICHER INDIAN MUSEUM GIFT SHOP
984 Lincoln Hts Ave
Ephrata, PA 17522-1542
Products: NA art

* FITCHS TRADING POST INC
230 N 3rd St
Harrisburg, PA 17101-1502
Products: NA merchandise

RHODE ISLAND

* DOVECREST INDIAN TRADING POST
Summit Rd
Exeter, RI 02822
Products: NA merchandise

* TURQUOISE, THE
Rockland Rd
N Scituate, Rl 02857
401-647-2579
Info: Send SASE
Products: SW jewelry, pottery, baskets, rugs, paintings, moccasins, clothing

* DOVE INDIAN TRADING POST
Main St
Rockville, RI 02873-9999
Products: NA merchandise

SOUTH CAROLINA

CANYON ROAD
1314 Celebrity Cir
Myrtle Beach, SC 29577
803-448-4880
Products: Original art, artifacts, masks, Navajo carvings, pottery, books, music, prints, jewelry

* WESTERN VISIONS INC
4728C Hwy 17 S N
Myrtle Beach
SC 29582-5355
803-272-2698
Products: Jewelry, fetishes, books, music, prints, sculpture, T-shirts, incense, art, artifacts, drums

* SARA AYERS
1182 Brockwood Cir
West Columbia
SC 29169-4006
803-794-5436
Price list: Send SASE
Products: Pottery pipes, vases, pitchers, canoes, candlesticks, bowls, jardinieres, cups, etc

SOUTH DAKOTA

* ALS OASIS
W Hwy 16
Chamberlain, SD 57325
Products: Indian items

COOLIDGE INN GIFT SHOP
HC 83 Box 78
Custer, SD 57730-9704
Products: NA items

* DAKOTA TRADING POST
18 N 5th St
Custer, SD 57730-1524
Products: NA merchandise

* DAKOTA SHOP
441 Mt Rushmore Rd
Custer, SD 57730-1530
Products: NA merchandise

* New listings, NA = Native American, SW = Southwest.

PIONEER TRADING POST
143 S Chicago
Hot Springs
SD 57747-2322
605-745-5252
Catalog: $5
Products: Buyers of old Indian and cowboy items, antiques of all kinds. Sales also

* CEDAR PASS LODGE
Badlands National Park
Interior, SD 57750
Products: NA merchandise

* BLACK HILLS SOUVENIRS & GIFTS
PO Box 670
Keystone, SD 57751-0670
Products: NA merchandise

* MAKOCE WANBLI
PO Box 184
Lower Brule
SD 57548-0184
605-343-0603
Info: Send SASE
Products: Traditional Plains NA art, clothing, dolls, weapons, clothing, moccasins, drums

* RINGS N THINGS
PO Box 360
Mission, SD 57555-0360
605-856-4548
Info: Send SASE
Products: Silver gifts, quillwork, beadwork

* KLEIN MUSEUM SHOP
W Hwy 12
Mobridge, SD 57601
Products: Indian artwork, hand crafts

* BRULE SIOUX ARTS AND CRAFTS COMPANY
PO Box 449
Saint Francis
SD 57572-0499
Products: NA art and crafts

* LONGHORN STORE
PO Box 32
19 Main St
Scenic, SD 57780-0032
605-993-4822
No catalog
Products: Lakota artifacts, buffalo skulls, robes, paintings, beadwork, costumes, quillwork, drums, more

* W H OVER GIFT SHOP
414 E Clark
Vermillion, SD
 57069-2307
Products: NA items

TENNESSEE

* ARIZONA ROOM
PO Box 751032
Memphis
TN 38175-1032
Products: NA merchandise

TEXAS

* NARANJOS WORLD OF AMERICAN INDIAN ART
PO Box 7973
Houston, TX 77270-7973
713-660-9690
Price list: Send SASE
Products: Jewelry, beadwork, leatherwork, pottery, baskets, rugs and dolls and Kachinas

* CROWS NEST ART GALLERY
230 Jefferson St
La Porte, TX 77571-6432
713-471-4371
Flyer: Free
Products: NA art, jewelry, and collectibles, Representing artisans from several tribes

* EAGLE DANCER
159 Gulf Fwy S
League City
TX 77573-3521
713-332-6028
Info: Send SASE
Products: Leatherwork, paintings, wood carvings, sculptures, jewelry, pottery, rugs, dolls

ART AND FRAME CO OF THE SOUTHWEST
14318 Angus St
San Antonio
TX 78247-1936
Products: Art, and frames

45

UTAH

* COW CANYON TRADING POST
PO Box 88
Bluff, UT 84512-0088
Products: NA merchandise

* BLUE MOUNTAIN TRADING POST
PO Box 263
Blanding
UT 84511-0263
Products: NA merchandiseox

KENNEDY INDIAN ARTS
PO Box 39
BIuff, UT 84512
505-343-1382
Products: Pottery, jewelry, rugs, fetishes, baskets, Kachinas; collections liquidated

* BRYCE CANYON LODGE
PO Box 371
Panguitch, UT 84759-0371
Products: NA merchandise

* ASHLEY TRADING POST
236 E Main St
Vernal, UT 84078-2606
Products: NA merchandise

VIRGINIA

* RED ROCK TRADING COMPANY
315 Cameron St
Alexandria
VA 22314-3219
Products: NA items

* BEAR CREEK TRADERS
PO Box 134
Amissville
VA 22002-0134
Products: NA items

SILVER PHOENIX
10610 Main St
Fairfax, VA 22030
Products: Jewelry, sandpaintings, pottery, Kachinas, rugs, moccasins, beadwork

WASHINGTON

* POTLATCH GIFTS
Northwind Trading Co
PO Box 217
Anacortes
WA 98221-0217
206-293-6404
Brochure: Send SASE
Products: Salish-style woodcarving and pottery, jewelry, baskets, clothing

SIDDHARA
Lyn Enterprises
PO Box 794
Camas, WA 98607
206-834-0817
Products: Silver and turquoise jewelry, beadwork, leathercraft

* COLVILLE TRIBAL MUSEUM GIFT SHOP
PO Box 233
Coulee Dam
WA 99116-1323
509-633-0751
Brochure: Available
Products: Powwow / flute cassettes, Pendleton / Hudson Bay blankets, Plateau Indian books
Prices: Call

* MAKAH CULTURAL RESEARCH CENTER
PO Box 160
Neah Bay
WA 98357-0160
206-645-2711
Price list: Send SASE
Products: Baskets, artifact replicas and wood masks, totem poles, rattles, bowls, shell jewelry

TRIBES
704 N 34th
Seattle, WA 98103
206-632-8842
Products: NA art, crafts, carvings, spirit masks, chokers and jewelry, more

---

* New listings, NA = Native American,
SW = Southwest.

* SOARING EAGLE TRADING POST
Rt 2 Box 26
St John, WA 99171
509-648-3743
Catalog: $5
Products: NA artifacts, bows and arrows, tomahawks, shields, medicine wheels, skulls, spears, more

* SONG STICK
PO Box 490
Chimacum, WA 98325
360-732-4279
Products: Beadwork, traditional flutes

* SUQUAMISH MUSEUM
PO Box 498
Suquamish
WA 98392-0498
360-598-3311
Price list: $2
Products: Beadwork, carvings, post/note cards, books, T-shirts, calendars, wood crafts

* BEAD LADY
Cherokee Rainbow
315 Roosevelt #B
Wenatchee
WA 98801-2944
Info: Send SASE
Products: Beadwork, moccasins, dance costumes, clothing

WISCONSIN

* BUFFALO BAY TRADING CO
PO Box 1350
Bayfield, Wl 54814-1350
Products: NA merchandise

* WA SWA GON ARTS & CRAFTS
PO Box 477
Lac Du Flambeau
Wl 54538-0477
715-588-7636
Info: Send SASE
Products: Beadwork, birch bark items, moccasins, fingerweaving, trad/ceremonial clothes

* KATY'S AMERICAN INDIAN ARTS
1817 Monroe St
Madison, Wl 53711-2024
608-251-5451
Products: Navajo, Zuni, Hopi jewelry, baskets, drums, music, sandpaintings, SW home decor

* MILWAUKEE PUBLIC MUSEUM SHOP GIFT SHOP
800 W Wills St
Milwaukee, Wl 53233
Products:

* WHITE THUNDER WOLF
320 E Clybourn St
Milwaukee, Wl 53202
414-278-7424
Catalog: $4
Products: Art, jewelry, drums, music, books, beads, supplies, crafts, gifts

* JO'S LOG CABIN TRADING POST
Box 294
4220 W Mason
Oneida, Wl 54155
414-869-2505
No catalog
Products: Silver, turquoise jewelry, quill boxes, custom leathering, dreamcatchers, crafts, more

* NATIVE AMERICAN CREATIONS
266 W Broadway
Waukesha, Wl 53186
414-549-7959
Products: Sterling silver, turquoise, beadwork, kachinas, pottery, leather crafts

47

* WINNEBAGO PUBLIC INDIAN MUSEUM

PO Box 441
Wisconsin Dells
WI 53965-0441
608-254-2268
Price list: $1
Products: Winnebago baskets, beadwork, deerskin products, pottery, rugs, silver items

WYOMING

* LA RAY TURQUOISE SHOP

PO Box 83
Cody, WY 82414-0083
307-587-9564
Brochure: Send SASE
Products: Navajo rugs, Ojibwa beadwork; Navajo, Zuni, Chippewa, and Hopi silver items

* MORNING STAR INDIAN GALLERY

PO Box 2343
Cody, WY 82414-2343
307-587-6577
Catalog: $3
Products: Craft supplies, prints, tapes, beadwork, pottery, sculptures, rugs

* WARM VALLEY ARTS & CRAFTS

PO Box 538
Fort Washakie
WY 82514-0157
Products: NA items

* BOYERS INDIAN ARTS & CRAFTS

PO Box 647
Jackson, WY 83001-0647
Products: NA merchandise

* WARBONNET

PO Box 3494
Jackson, WY 83001-3494
800-950-0154
Catalog: Free
Products: 75 tribes represented, rugs, flutes, baskets, dream catchers, pottery, jewelry, more

* DORNANS GIFT SHOP

#10 Moose St
Moose, WY 83012
Products: NA merchandise

* WIND RIVER TRADING CO

US Hwy 287 Ft
Washakie, WY 82514
307-332-3267
Fax: 307-332-6962
Products: Eastern Shoshone and Northern Arapahoe beadwork, books, tapes, herbs, supplies

CANADA

ARCTIC CO-OPERATIVES LTD

1645 Inkster Blvd
Winnipeg, Manitoba
Canada R2X 2W7
204-697-1880
Products: Marketing and special events coordinator; Inuit and Dene arts and crafts

QUILLWORK BY BRENT BOYD

Box 251
Williamsburg, Ontario
Canada K0C 2H0
613-535-2233
Products: Quillwork

* New listings, NA = Native American, SW = Southwest.

Contemporary Crafts and Southwestern Home Accessories

ALASKA

* **MARDINA DOLLS**
PO Box 611
Wrangell, AK 99929-0611
Info: Send long SASE
Products: Eskimo dolls
in ceremonial robes

ARKANSAS

**GARBERS CRAFTED
LIGHTING**
Rt 2 Box 140
Mammoth Spring
AR 72554
501-966-4996
Catalog: $4
Products: Painted
punched-tin Texas long-
horn lamp, several west-
ern/SW designs

ARIZONA

**BIG HORN
COLLECTIBLES**
PO Box 1477
Chandler, AZ 85244
602-303-9494
Catalog: $3
Products: Metal drawer
pulls, lamp finials, cur-
tain rods, curtain swags,
western/wildlife motifs

AIRDANCE
PO Box 2090
Chino Valley
AZ 86323
520-636-2759
Brochure: $2.50
Products: SW leather
shields or mandalas, air-
brushed with cow skull
or wolf designs

**CATTLE COMPANY
RANCH HOUSE**
PO Box 27
Elfrida, AZ 85610
520-824-3540
Catalog: $2
Products: Western din-
nerware sets and flat-
ware, napkins, glass-
ware

* **GIFT SHOP OF
JEROME**
PO Box 396
Jerome, AZ 86331-0396
Products: Indian art,
crafts

**SOUTHWEST
IMAGES**
Chambers & Chambers
9403 Charwood Dr
Oklahoma City
AZ 73139
405-793-0130
Products: SW-style
stucco bird houses,
crafted from pine;
miniature blankets,
accessories

**WHITES WESTERN
IRONWORKS**
43809 N Coyote Rd
Queen Creek, AZ 85242
602-987-0307
Products: Handcrafted
lamps and tables, SW
themes

* **GIFTS GALORE**
273 N Hwy 89A, Ste A
Sedona, AZ 86336-4242
Products: NA hand-
crafts

* **GORDON
WHEELERS TRADING
POST**
201 Hwy 279
Sedona, AZ 86336-6113
Products: Indian hand-
crafts, art

**TRES AMIGOS
TRADERS**
771 Catalina Dr
Sierra Vista, AZ 85635
520-458-0769
Brochure: Free
Products: Glazed west-
ern style bathroom sink;
horseshoe lamps; copper
lampshades

AK DESIGNS
PO Box 41572
Tucson, AZ 85717
520-323-3282
Brochure: $3
Products: Handmade,
hand etched lamps and
mirrors, pottery lamps,
SW, NA, and country
styles

* New listings, NA = Native American,
SW = Southwest.

SONORAN GLASS KRAFTS
PO Box 27522
Tucson, AZ 85726
800-KRAFTS-1
Products: Stained glass rista pepper clock, and cowboy boot clock, signed/numbered/dated

ZINGERS
PO Box 30087
Tucson, AZ 85751-0087
800-891-8654
Products: Copper fetish ornaments, Kokopelli, cactus, coyote, bear, horse, tortoise, rabbit designs

STIX & STONES
2490 Yowell Ct #52
Yuma, AZ 85364
520-783-3032
Brochure: $2
Products: Terra cotta Choctaw made spirit wall masks

CALIFORNIA

* **COWBOYS & INDIANS**
3225 Willow Glen
Orcutt, CA 93455-2362
805-937-7535
Products: NA items

DESERT DREAMS ETC
40-100 Washington St
Bermuda Dunes
CA 92201
619-360-8860
Brochure: $2
Products: Rough-sawn cedar boxes and assorted Western gifts

* **DESERT TRADER, THE**
PO Box 328
Whitethorn
CA 95589-0328
Products: Native American items

* **INDIAN STORE, THE**
PO Box 308
Los Gatos
CA 95031-0308
Products: Native American art and crafts

PIECEMAKERS COUNTRY STORE
1720 Adams Ave
Costa Mesa, CA 92626
714-641-3112
Catalog: $2
Products: Country crafts in Colorado, and California. "Everything from A to Z"

* **ONE SQUAW ENTERPRISES**
1286 Discovery St #106
San Marcos
CA 92069-4045
Products: NA items

PATRICKS
Box 323
Clovis, CA 93613
Catalog: $2
Products: Drums, handmade paper, 3D cards, vinegar

* **RUNNING STREAM CREATIONS**
10414 Fernglen
Tujunga, CA 91042
818-352-5480
No catalog
Products:
Dreamcatchers, shields, medicine wheels, earrings from shell, bone, gems, fetishes

* **SILVERADO GLASS STUDIO**
PO Box 274
Silverado Canyon
CA 92676
714-649-2626
Photos/Price list: Available
Products: Native American stained glass home accessories

COLORADO

MYERS AND COMPANY
1025, 555 Basalt Ave
Basalt, CO 81621
970-927-4761
Brochure: Call
Products: Hand-forged iron wall sconces, rawhide shade

AMERICAN HERITAGE CRAFTS
PO Box 330
Delta, CO 81416
970-874-0706
Catalog: $2
Products: Western and country style whirlygigs

DENVER HARDWARE
3200 Walnut St
Denver, CO 80205
303-292-3550
Products: Western and country style door hardware, other hardware

WHOHS SHOWROOMS
2900 E 6th Ave at Filmore
Denver, CO 80206
303-321-3232
Products: Country kitchens, Appliances, etc.

SOUTHWEST COUNTRY
PO Box 1204
Evergreen, CO 80439
800-373-0391
Catalogs and brochures: $12
Products: Sw, western, mountain lamps, chandeliers, wall sconces, made of iron, ceramic, antler, etc.

ANTLER ART
PO Box 2006
Grand Junction
CO 81502-2006
970-243-5114
Brochure: Free
Products: All types of antler chandeliers and furniture.

TUMBLEWEED
PO Box 775856
Steamboat Springs
CO 80477
970-879-0105
Products: Handcrafted SW pueblo clock, sand-textured finish.

* COLLECTORS ROOM
PO Box 3226
Vail, CO 80657
Products: Native American items.

WOLF CREATIONS
8269 Rd F
Wiggins, CO 80654
970-432-5208
Products: Horseshoe wall hooks, western style.

DELWARE

HAT-SKETS BY TWO SISTERS
Rt 1 Box 337-A
Seaford, DE 19973
302-629-9119/0386
Products: SW gift-filled hats, handcrafted/painted usables, edibles and keepsakes.

FLORIDA

PITTS, THE
PO Box 264
Loughman, FL 33858
407-396-0036
Products: Handcarved and painted pottery, gold inlay, Kokopelli, desert, and humming bird designs.

LUCKY HORSESHOE ART INC
1846 NW 54th Ave
Margate, FL 33063
305-969-0810
Brochure: $2
Products: Cowboy business-card holder and bareback rider, made with horseshoes.

* DREAM CATCHERS
5401 S Kirkman Rd
Ste 680
Orlando, FL 32819-7912
Products: Native American merchandise.

---

* New listings, NA = Native American,
SW = Southwest.

B & R CERAMICS
757 Snead Cir West
Palm Beach, FL 33413
407-471-0311
Products: Ceramics.

SANTA FE TRADING CO
12999 144th
Palm Beach Gardens
FL 33418
407-622-6911
Catalog: $5
Products: Rustic,
heavy-gauge metal
home hardware, western/NA images; mirrors.

MANY MOONS
2929 Hwy 60 W
Plant City, FL 33567-1607
Brochure: $3
Products: Copper wall
sculptures, western/NA
theme decor.

GEORGIA

**MOOSEHEAD LODGE
AT BLUE RIDGE
ANTIQUES MALL**
Main St & Depot St
Blue Ridge, GA 30513
706-632-5549
Products: SW leather
pillows, primitive furniture, Kiva ladders, decorative accessories.

LUXURIES BY LYNNA
Rt 1 Box 2634
Tiger, GA 30576
706-782-5124
Products: China plates with
NA & wildlife designs.

IDAHO

**NORTHWEST METAL
DESIGNS**
PO Box 527
Rathdrum, ID 83858
208-687-2588
Dealer inquiries welcome.
Products: Northwest-style metal art and rustic home furnishings.

ILLINOIS

**COUNTRY STORE OF
GENEVA**
28 James St
Geneva, IL 60134
708-879-0098
Catalog: $2
Products: Mulberry
chandeliers.

**COWBOYS &
OUTLAWS**
117 E Sangamon Ave
Rantail, IL 61866
217-893-1457
Brochure: Free
Products: Amethyst
and pewter figurines,
designs such as coyote,
horses, SW.

INDIANA

*** INDIAN AFFAIRS
TRADING CO**
3405 N Virginia Ave
Muncie, IN 47304-1878
Products: Native merchandise.

IOWA

**LORRAINES DOLL
CLOSET**
23503 Glacier Rd
Sioux City, IA 51108
800-257-7568
Products: Porcelain
Indian dolls buckskin
costume, britches, moccasins, stand, pelt.

KANSAS

WILDFLOWERS
PO Box 350
Derby, KS 67037
316-788-9337
Products: Handmade
boxes with leather,
cowhide, antlers.

**AMERICAN MEDIA
GROUP**
7300 W 110th St Ste 960
Overland Park
KS 66210
913-345-9987
Brochure: Free
Products: "Totem
Stones," and
"Foundation Stones."
Animals images carved
into stones.

MINNESOTA

SOUTHWEST CONNECTION
5005 France Ave S
Minneapolis, MN 55410
612-924-0787
Products: SW home accessories, war clubs, fountains, ceramics, jewelry, saguaro cactus crafts.

MONTANA

COUNTRY CABIN DESIGNS
Box 415
Crow Agency, MT 59022
406-638-4458
Brochure: $3
Products: Pine/rope western-style magazine rack; wall clock crafted in cultured marble.

ARCHITECTURAL ART GLASS
PO Box 1104
Helena, MT 59624
406-443-6644
Products: Glass and window etching artist.

ATLANTIS SUN
1010 2nd Rd NE
Power, MT 59468
406-467-2901
Products: Bronze rodeo statues on wooden bases.

NEBRASKA

* ABBY'S WILD ROSE
315 Box Butte Ave
Alliance, NE 69301-3341
Products: Indian items.

BRICKSTONE STUDIOS
2108 S 38th St
Lincoln, NE 68506
800-449-6599
Products: Handcrafted sculpture of wildlife and birds of prey.

NEVADA

* INDIAN TRADING POST
PO Box 671
Virginia City
NV 89440-0671
Products: Native American art and crafts.

NEW JERSEY

LEWIS & CLARK COLLECTION
23 Longview Rd
Cedar Grove, NJ 07009
201-239-6480
Brochure: $1
Products: Leather journals, albums and picture frames and mirrors.

LLOYDS 5TH AVENUE
310 Crosby Ave
Deal, NJ 07723
908-531-2332
Products: "Cheyenne flatware," "Adirondack Stoneware" dining sets.

NEW MEXICO

JULIE HOPKINS STUDIO
PO Box 81192
Albuquerque
NM 87198-1192
505-266-8248
Brochure: $3.50
Products: SW wall decor, padded, painted suede dolls

HIGH MOUNTAIN WOODWORKS
PO Box 2108
Edgewood, NM 87015
505-281-7876
Products: SW home accessories, clocks, magazine racks, napkin holders, lamps, salt & pepper, etc

DESERT COUNTRY DESIGNS
PO Box 7792
Las Cruces, NM 88006
505-524-3233
Products: Desert motif fabric baskets

EARTHKEEPER
PO Box 304
Montezuma, NM 87731
Products: NA supplies

* New listings, NA = Native American, SW = Southwest.

CUSTOM IRONWARE
560 Montezuma
Santa Fe, NM 87501
505-988-3348
Call to find a dealer
near you
Products: Handcrafted
iron home decor iron
hardware, western and
country styles

**SOUTHWESTERN
LIGHT**
PO Box 548
Santa Fe, NM 87504
505-473-1077
Catalog: $5
Products: Santa Fe style
hand thrown pottery
light fixtures, 60 styles,
10 natural clay colors

**SEAGULL
CREATIONS**
222 Calais
Tijeras, NM 87059
505-286-1253
Brochure: $2
Products: SW switch
covers, hand painted
ceramic; bathroom
accessories available

NEW YORK

PETER B JONES
PO Box 174
Versailles
NY 14168-0174
716-532-5993
Info: Send SASE
Products: Original
works in clay, one-of-a-
kind ceramic sculptures,
and wall hangings

NORTH CAROLINA

**FRISCO NATIVE
AMERICAN MUSEUM**
Hwy 12/Sunset Strip
Frisco, NC 27936
919-995-4440
Products:
Dreamcatchers incorpor-
ating seahorses, starfish,
other ocean-found
objects

**HUNT GALLERIES
INC**
PO Box 2324
Hickory, NC 28063
800-248-3876
Brochure: Free
Products: Custom
upholstered furniture,
love seats, sofas, chaise
lounges, chairs, benches,
more

OHIO

**BLACK SWAMP
WAGONWORKS**
PO Box 55
Swanton, OH 43558
Products: Models of
chuck wagons and
Conestogas, hay wag-
ons, and grain wagons,
unassembled

OKLAHOMA

* INDIAN STORE
2315 E Cherokee St
Sallisaw, OK 74955-5450
Products: Native
American art and crafts

**RUSTIC WESTERN
DESIGNS**
12601 Natasha Way
Yukon, OK 73099-9704
405-373-1838
Products: Handmade
rustic western mirror,
crafted from barn wood,
trimmed in harness
leather

OREGON

*** LAUGHING
MALLARD**
29765 Gimpi Way
Eugene, OR 97402
541-485-5007
Products: Makers of
"The Oregon Flute
Quiver," protection for
flutes

55

**PENDLETON
COWGIRL CO**
PO Box 30142
Eugene, OR 97403
541-484-9194
Catalog: $2
Products: Western T-
shirts, lithographs, cal-
endars, note card sets

* **LAR KING
ENTERPRISES**
815 E 13th
McMinnville
OR 97128-3733
541-434-5165
Products: Custom
sewing, and chalked
ceramics

NATIVEWORK
2534 North 20th
Springfield, OR 97477
541-0727
Catalog: None
Products: Etched
stones; dream catchers

PENNSYLVANIA

PUEBLO TRADERS
Box 261-B
Dallas, PA 18612
717-639-5957
Products: Ceramic
gourd rattles, snake
dream catchers

CHESTNUT HILL
511 W King St
East Berlin, PA 17316
717-259-7502
Products: Antique
reproduction home fur-
nishings

**CHARLIES GIRL
LIGHTING**
1448 Street Rd
New Hope, PA 18938
215-598-7571
Catalog: $3
Products: Colonial
reproductions of chan-
deliers and lighting

*SOUTH
DAKOTA*

* **DIANNES GIFT
CORRAL AND
HILLYO MUSEUM**
Star Rt 63
Hill City, SD 57745
Products: Native
American merchandise

TEXAS

**NORTH PASS
CREATIONS INC**
9282 Montana Ave
El Paso, TX 79925
915-598-9065
Products: SW style
ceramic canister sets,
table accessories, night
lights

**CHEROKEE HEART
ART AND TEES**
PO Box 308
San Augustine
TX 75972
Brochure: $3
Products: Mandalas,
masks, dreamcatchers,
T-shirts

**OSBORN
COLLECTION INC,
THE**
25818 Budde Rd
Spring, TX 77380
713-298-6562
Products: SW decora-
tive terra cotta ceramics,
trimmed with feathers
and raffia

**SMITH FURNITURE
COMPANY**
4326 Tejasco
San Antonio, TX 78218
210-822-2112
Products: Decorative
stools and ottomans

WASHINGTON

**WINTERHAWK
GALLERY**
N 36108 Conklin Rd
Elk, WA 99009
800-793-6505
Products: Western style
mailbox holder & ranch-
sign plant hanger,
wildlife, horses themes

* New listings, NA = Native American,
SW = Southwest.

56

HANG EM HIGH
6260 139th NE #94
Redmond, WA 98052
206-883-2009
Brochure: $2
Products:
Leather/ceramic tree
ornaments, keychains,
car ornaments, SW/NA

* **WILY COYOTE**
2917 N Stout Rd
Spokane
WA 99206-4318
Products: NA items

WEST VIRGINIA

D & S CERAMICS
300 Broadway Ave
Parkersburg, WV 26101
304-485-8977
Products: Handpainted
SW ceramics; figurines,
lamps, vases, masks,
wall hangings, more

* **END OF THE TRAIL ll**
2200 Centre Market
Wheeling, WV 26003
614-277-3280
304-277-3280
Products: Indian items

WISCONSIN

AMERICAN INDIAN SHOP
544 E Ogden Ave
Milwaukee, Wl 53202
414-964-0720
Products: Custom
works of art, from turtle
shells to bentwood
shields, neck and ear
wear

WYOMING

BARBS OF THE WEST
PO Box 1167
Big Piney, WY 83113
307-276-5717
Brochure: $1
Products: Rustic
barbed-wire designs
with western flare;
boots, brands, signs, etc

WESTERN HERITAGE
1301 Rawhide Dr
Gillette, WY 82716
307-682-1347
Brochure: Available
Products: Rattles made
with horse hair, antler,
rawhide, glass beads;
plain, or fur optional
custom

Textiles, Rugs, Blankets

GENERAL LISTINGS

THE FARIBAULT WOOLEN MILL CO
800-448 9665
Products: Bear-design blanket form the "Wellspring Collection"

KAREN WIGHT TEXTURE DESIGN RESOURCES
505-982-9746
Products: Rugs of all kinds

MOUNTAIN MULES AND COUNTRY QUILTS
307-587-5013
Info: Call
Products: Pieced quilts, with wild life and western themes

ARIZONA

BOUCHER BOYS & THE INDIAN
5230 Via Buena Vista
Paradise Valley
AZ 85253
602-948-2423
Products: Pima Indian designed Indian-print blankets

CALIFORNIA

ANOMALY IMPORTS TRADING POST
3210 State st
Santa Barbara, CA 93105
Products: SW basketry, rugs, stools

ILLINOIS

INDIAN ART UNLTD
Wanda Campbell RT 1
Box 283
Cami, IL 62821
Products: Navajo wavings

MICHIGAN

THE CACTUS COMPANY
2015 7th St.
Bay City, MI 48708
Products: 100% cotton textiles, rugs, throws, jackets, 108 different western patterns

MISSOURI

* MAHOTA HANDWOVENS
614 Hampton Place
Joplin, MO 64801-1009
Products: Native textiles

MONTANA

O BAR V
818 9th St SW
Sideny, MT 59270
406-482-3865
Products: "Quillows" with wildlife prints

NEW JERSEY

COURISTAN ADV DEPT
2 Executive Drive
Fort Lee, NJ 07024
800-223-6186
Color brochure: Phone
Products: NA design rugs

NEW MEXICO

ALEXANIAN RUGS, INC
3341 Columbia NE
Albuquerque, NM 87107
505-881-3333
Products: NA rugs

JAMES REID, LTD
Santa Fe, NM
505-988-1147
Products: Navajo textiles

* New listings, NA = Native American, SW = Southwest.

* QUILTS LTD
652 Canyon Rd
Santa Fe
NM 87501-2722
505-988-5888
Products:
Contemporary quilts,
antique quilts, wearable
art, jewelry, pillows,
quilt prints

**SAKIESTEWA
TEXTILES LTD**
PO Box 9337
Santa Fe
NM 87504-9337
800-230-4049
Catalog: Phone
Products: "Ancient
Blanket Series" of blan-
kets designed by Hopi
artist Ramona
Sakiestewa

NEW YORK

**5TH AVE RUG
CENTER**
366 5th Ave
New York, NU 10001
800-642-9108
Products: SW design
rugs

NORTH CAROLINA

**KIMBERLY BLACK
RUGS AND
ACCESSORIES**
PO Box 47927
Charlotte, NC 28247
800-296-6099
Catalogs: $5
Products: Flat-braid
and flat-woven rugs

TEXAS

**EL PASO SADDLE-
BLANKET CO
601 N Oregon
El Paso, TX 79901
915-544-1000
Catalog: Free
Products:** Indian made
and Mexican blankets,
rugs, pillows, placemats,
more

WASHINGTON

*** NATIVE TO NATIVE
ARTS AND CRAFTS**
PO Box 1719
Port Angeles
WA 98362-0087
800-457-5010
Products: Wool
"Waterbird" blankets,
designed by Larry Yazie

CANADA

*** KERMODE
MARKETING**
PO Box 1213
Winnipeg, MB R3C 2Y4
Canada
Products: Native textile
work

---

* New listings, NA = Native American,
SW = Southwest.

Finished Jewelry

and Silverwork

ALASKA

*** CAPTAIN COOK
FINE JEWELRY**
Hotel Captain Cook Ste E
Anchorage, AK 99501
Products: NA jewelry

*** FRED MEYER
JEWELERS**
Fifth Ave Mall
Anchorage, AK 99501
Products: NA jewelry

*** CHILKAT VALLEY
ARTS**
PO Box 125
Haines, AK 99827-0145
Price list: Send long SASE
Products: NW Coast
Tlinget NA silver jewelry

ARIZONA

*** LAWSONS
JEWELERS**
Main St
Camp Verde, AZ 86322
Products: NA jewelry

*** GLEAHS INDIAN
JEWELRY**
901 N Main Old Town
Cottonwood, AZ 86326
Products: NA jewelry

*** ABRAHAM BEGAYS
INDIAN JEWELRY**
17½ N Leroux
Flagstaff, AZ 86001-5540
Products: NA jewelry

*** DEES EXQUISITE
JEWELRY**
PO Box 235
Fredonia, AZ 86022-0235
Products: NA jewelry

*** MORNING STAR
INDIAN JEWELRY**
PO Box 987
Kingman
AZ 86402-0987
Products: Indian jewelry

*** FERRELLS INDIAN
JEWELRY**
269 N Hwy 89A
Sedona, AZ 86336-4218
Products: NA jewelry

*** GARLANDS INDIAN
JEWELRY**
PO Box 1848
Sedona, AZ 86339-1848
Products: NA jewelry

*** GODBERS JEWELRY
INC**
6900 E Camelback Rd
Scottsdale
AZ 85251-2431
Products: NA jewelry

**EAGLE MOUNTAIN
TURQUOISE
COMPANY**
8430 Golf Links
Tucson, AZ 85730
602-296-1090
Info: Free
Products: Sterling and
turquoise jewelry

Q C TURQUOISE
3340 E Washington
Phoenix, AZ 85034
602-267-1164
Info: Free
Products: Turquoise
nugget jewelry, nuggets
by the pound or strand,
and cutting material

CALIFORNIA

* DELUNA JEWELERS
521 2nd St
Davis, CA 95616-4618
Products: NA jewelry

* AB-ORIGINALS
PO Box 850
Trinidad, CA 95570-0850
707-677-3738
No mail order
Products: Fashion
accessories made from
shells, nuts, quills, bone,
berries, beads, etc

**BLUE SKY COMPANY,
THE**
10877 San Gabriel Way
Valley Center, CA 92082
Products: Sterling silver
jewelry, running horses,
western style, and
turquoise hearts

ZUNI PUEBLO
222 A Main St
Venice, CA 90291
Products: Zuni jewelry,
pottery, Fetishes, room
screens, paintings, hand-
made by Zuni artisans

* New listings, NA = Native American,
SW = Southwest.

DELAWARE

SECOND LOOK Silver Works Inc
3234 B Kirkwood Hwy
Wilmington, DE 19808
800-544-8200
Catalog: Free
Products:
Silver/turquoise earrings, bracelets, necklaces, watch bands and SW jewelry

FLORIDA

* **GREENS RINGS & THINGS**
PO Box 129
Everglades City
FL 33929-0129
Products: NA-inspired jewelry

ILLINOIS

* **GALL SOUTHWEST SILVER JEWELRY CO**
9014 3st St
Brookfield, IL 60513-1347
Products: NA jewelry

MARYLAND

JEWELRY BY AVERY
5134 Chalk Point Rd
West River, MD 20778
410-867-4752
Info: Send SASE
Products: NA art, precious and semi-precious gemstones, mineral specimens, NA jewelry

MASSACHUSETTS

NATURES JEWELRY
222 Mill Rd
Chelmsford, MA 01824
800-333-3235
Catalog: Free
Products: Leaves, shells, other natural objects transformed into jewelry, in precious metals

* **COURNEYS CUSTOM DESIGN JEWELRY**
754 Main St
Osterville
MA 02655-1904
Products: NA jewelry

MISSISSIPPI

BULL RUN
1407 Wooded Dr
Grenada, MS 38901
601-226-9292
Brochure: $3
Products: Sterling silver hand crafted jewelry

NEVADA

* **BRUNOS TURQUOISE**
106 Nevada Hwy
Boulder City
NV 89005-2643
Products: Sterling silver and turquoise Indian jewelry

* **JEWELERS AT DEL RIO**
PO Box 79
Verdi, NV 89439-0079
Products: NA jewelry

NEW JERSEY

* **MOON LAKE INDIAN JEWELRY**
175 Hayes Dr
Saddle Brook
NJ 07663-5016
Products: Indian jewelry

NEW MEXICO

* **CARLISLE SILVER CO INC**
PO Box 26627
Albuquerque
NM 87125-6627
Products: Navajo silver

* **DISTINCTIVE INDIAN JEWELRY**
1028 Stuart Rd NW
Albuquerque
NM 87114-1928
Products: NA jewelry

* **HILLS INDIAN JEWELRY INC**
3004 2nd St NW
Albuquerque
NM 87107-1418
Products: NA jewelry

* **FELIX INDIAN JEWELRY**
PO Box 195
Gallup, NM 87305-0195
Products: NA jewelry

* BROWNS TURQUOISE SHOP
224 W Coal Ave
Gallup, NM 87301-6306
Products: Navajo sterling silver and turquoise jewelry

DOPASO JEWELRY
PO Box 35430
Albuquerque, NM 87176
800-992-5234
Info: Free
Products: SW-style turquoise and sterling silver pins

* MILAINES SANTA FE SILVER
2030 Ridgecrest Dr SE
Albuquerque
NM 87108-4531
Products: Silver products

SURRISI TIMEPIECES MA & MC Corporation
PO Box 30094
2111 Church St
Albuquerque, NM 87104
505-888-0001
505-244-3045
Products: Watches with NA art on dial faces

ED YOUNGS INC, THE
PO Box 866
Belen, NM 87002
505-864-1242
Products: Wholesale Indian and SW jewelry and handcrafts

TWIN FEATHER DESIGNS
PO Box 275
Gallup, NM 87305
505-722-5792
Products: Earrings in sterling silver and tufa stone sandcasting; Navajo artist

* KASTENBIECKS INDIAN JEWELRY
831 E Santa Fe Ave
Grants, NM 87020-2458
Products: NA jewelry

ANDY LEE KIRK
PO Box 460
Isleta, NM 87022
505-869-6098
Products: Specializing in gold and silver Indian jewelry

550 SILVER & SUPPLY Monsterslayer Inc
PO Box 550
Kirtland, NM 87417
505-598-5332
Products: Metals, stones, beads, Findings, jewelers and supplies; handmade Navajo jewelry

MICHAEL WIGLEY GALLERIES LTD
1111 Paseo de Peralta
Santa Fe, NM 87501
505-984-8986
Products: NA jewelry and paintings

SURRISI TIMEPIECES MA & MC Corporation
66 E San Francisco St #9
Santa Fe, NM 87501
505-893-7666
Products: Watches with NA art on dial faces

ERIACHO ARTS & CRAFTS
PO Box 912
Zuni, NM 87327-0912
505-782-2122
Products: Artists of traditional Zuni inlay jewelry

ZUNI INDIAN JEWELRY Silver Bear Jewelry
Drawer F
Pia Mesa Rd #32
Zuni, NM 87327
505-782-2869/505-870-7027
Products: Zuni jewelry

* New listings, NA = Native American,
SW = Southwest.

NEW YORK

* LITTLE FEATHER TRADING POST
PO Box 3165
Jamaica, NY 11431-3165
212-658-0576
Info: Send SASE
Products: Beadwork and silver jewelry and leatherwork

APL TRADER
PO Box 1900
New York, NY 10185
813-870-3180
Price list: $1
Products: Precious and semi precious gem-stones, carvings, beads

KOKOPELLI Southwestern Jewelry
120 Thompson St
New York, NY 10012
212-925-4411
Products: Contemporary and tra-ditional NA jewelry and hand crafted fetishes

NORTH CAROLINA

* GWIN-SOUTHWEST
4004 South Blvd
Charlotte, NC 28209
704-527-8388 ext 18
Flyer: Free
Products: Handmade Am Indian sterling sil-ver and gold jewelry

OHIO

AMERICAN SILVER FROM THE SOUTHWEST
5700 Frederick Rd
Dayton, OH 45414
513-890-0138
Info: Free
Products: NA and con-temporary jewelry, pot-tery, and Kachinas

OKLAHOMA

* DANCING RABBIT
814 N Jones Ave
Norman, OK 73069-7714
405-360-0512
Info: Send SASE
Products: Contemporary jewelry and beadweavings

* SNAKE CREEK WORKSHOP
PO Box 147
Rose, OK 74364-0147
918-479-8867
Brochure: Send SASE
Products: Mussel shell gorget necklaces

OREGON

GUYOT ARTS
2945 SE 140th St
Portland, OR 97236
503-761-9519
Brochure: Send SASE
Products: Original ster-ling silver naturalistic-and abstract-theme jew-elry

RHODE ISLAND

J H BREAKELL AND COMPANY
69 Mill St
Newport, Rl 02840
800-767-6411
Catalog: $2
Products: Handcrafted sterling silver and 14K gold jewelry

SOUTH DAKOTA

* LAKOTA JEWELRY CREATIONS
909 E St Patrick St Ste 16
Rapid City
SD 57701-5720
605-343-0603
Catalog: $2
Products: Sterling silver jewelry, jewelry with inlays of stones, or trimmed with gold, brass, copper

TENNESSEE

DES HANDMADE CRAFTS
112 Randy Rd
Madison, TN 37115
615-868-5279
Brochure: Free
Products: Handcrafted clay jewelry

TEXAS

CIRCLE D JEWELRY
9440 McCombs St
El Paso, TX 79924
915-755-4479
Catalog: $2
Products: Sterling silver
and 14K jewelry

*** INDIAN CREEK
JEWELRY**
601 Brown Tr #106
Hurst, TX 76053-5743
Products: NA jewelry

VERMONT

**TURKEY MOUNTAIN
INDIAN ARTS**
PO Box 231
Jamaica, VT 05343
802-874-4564
By appointment
Products: NA jewelry

WYOMING

**BLACK DIAMOND
JEWELERS**
PO Box 6285
Jackson Hole, WY 83001
800-733-7798
Products: Western style
jewelry

* A & P PAWN SHOP
214 West Main St
Lander, WY 82520-3128
Products: NA pawn
jewelry, other NA items

WASHINGTON

ZUNI INDIAN SILVER
Lynwood, WA 98036
206-778-9274
Products: Handmade
Indian jewelry Zuni
Indian silver; turquoise
craftsman, specialty
inlay / channel work

* New listings, NA = Native American,
SW = Southwest.

Native American
Craftmaking Supplies

ALABAMA

* INDIAN CAMP CREEK HANDICRAFTS
RR 1 Box 278A
Florence, AL 35630-9366
205-766-8184
Catalog: $2
Products: NA cornhusk dolls, miniature hand-carved gourd vessels

ALASKA

* IVORY BROKER
817 W 6th Ave
Anchorage
AK 99501-2045
Products: Ivory

* BEADS N THINGS
PO Box 1897
Fairbanks, AK 99707
Products: Beads and supplies

ARIZONA

ARROW GEMS AND MINERALS
PO Box 9068
Phoenix, AZ 85068
602-997-6373
Catalog: Free
Products: Pewter figurines, pendants, buckles, beads, findings, mineral specimens, gemstones

MOHAVE INDUSTRIES INC
2365 Northern Ave
Kingman, AZ 86401
602-757-2480
Brochure: $1
Products: Lapidary equipment

HARDIES
PO Box 1920
Quartzsite, AZ 85346
602-927-6381
Catalog: $3
Products: Beads, findings, buckles and bolas, NA jewelry, gems, rocks, and books

ARC TRADERS
Box 3429
Scottsdale, AZ 85257
602-945-0769
Info: Free
Products: Findings, chains, earrings, sterling silver, gold filled and 14K gold beads

KIKICO BEADS
PO Box 8353
Scottsdale, AZ 85252
602-953-2728
Catalog: $2
Products: Beads for jewelry design

AMBASSADOR
PO Box 28807
Tucson, AZ 85076
602-748-8600
Catalog: Free
Products: Cloisonne, turquoise, sterling silver, precious and semi precious gemstones

DISCOUNT AGATE HOUSE
3401 N Dodge Blvd
Tucson, AZ 85716
602-323-0781
Info: Free
Products: Rocks and minerals from around the world; lapidary equipment, sterling silver, findings

CALIFORNIA

JARVI TOOL COMPANY
1200 E Debra Ln
Anaheim, CA 92805
714-774-9104
Info: Free
Products: Lapidary equipment, faceting machines, other tools

VICTOR H LEW INC
1355 S Flower St
Los Angeles, CA 90015
213-749-8247
Catalog: $5
Products: Findings, gemstones, jewelry-making supplies

* New listings, NA = Native American, SW = Southwest.

COTTON BALL, THE
475 Morro Bay Blvd
Morro Bay, CA 94332
Catalog: $3
Products: Charms, ornaments, kits and findings, books, jewelry making supplies

CREATIVE CASTLE
2372 Michael Dr
Newbury Park
CA 91320
805-499-1377
Catalog: Free
Products: Bead-making jewelry kits

AMBER COMPANY, THE
5643 Cahuenga Blvd
North Hollywood
CA 91601
818-509-5730
Price list: Free
Products: Amber specimens, beads, fossils, jewelry, books, lapidary supplies

EMBELLISHMENTS FOR DESIGNING PEOPLE
4793 Telegraph Ave
Oakland, CA 94609
510-436-6415
Catalog: $2
Products: Charms, stampings, books, tools, findings

TERRIFIC LITTLE CRAFTS
4140 Oceanside Blvd
Oceanside, CA 92056
Catalog: $1
Products: Jewelry findings, quilling and other craft supplies, and paper clay

COVINGTON ENGINEERING CORPORATION
PO Box 35
Redlands, CA 92373
714-793-6636
Catalog: Free
Products: Lapidary equipment

ULTRA TEC
1025 E Chestnut
Santa Ana, CA 92701
714-542-0608
Brochure: Free
Products: Lapidary equipment

TIERRACAST
3177 Guerneville Rd
Santa Rosa, CA 95401
707-545-5787
Catalog: Free
Products: Jewelry making supplies

GEMSTONE EQUIPMENT MANUFACTURING CO
750 Easy St
Simi Valley, CA 93065
805-527-6990
Info: Free
Products: Tumblers and other lapidary equipment

RISING ARROW
265-M Sobrante Way
Sunnyvale
CA 94086-4809
408-732-2001
Catalog: $1
Products: Beads, hides, furs, feathers, bone hairpipe, and other NA craft supplies

CONTEMPO LAPIDARY
12257 Foothill Blvd
Sylmar, CA 91342
818-899-1973
Brochure: Free
Products: Lapidary equipment

CGM INC
19562 Ventura Blvd
Tarzana, CA 91356
818-609-7088
Catalog: Free
Products: Precious and semi precious gemstones; sterling silver findings

69

COLORADO

HORSEFEATHERS OF ASPEN
300 Puppysmith Rd
Aspen, CO 81611
970-925-1890
Brochure: $5
Products: Specialty knobs and pulls for your mountain home; cabinet and furniture hardware

ACKLEYS ROCKS AND STAMPS
3230 N Stone Ave
Colorado Springs
CO 80907
719-633-1153
Catalog: $1
Products: Lapidary and silver smithing supplies, mountings, and findings

PIKES PEAK ROCK SHOP
1316 Pecan St
Colorado Springs
CO 80904
800-347-6257
Catalog: Free
Products: Fossils, crystals, stones and agates, amethyst, beads, stands

CONNECTICUT

NGRAVER COMPANY, THE
67 Wawecus Hill Rd
Bozrah, CT 06334
203-823-1533
Catalog: $1
Products: Engraving tools and jewelry-making equipment

NEYCRAFT
Division of Ney
Ney Industrial Park
Bloomfield, CT 06002
800-5384593
Info: Free
Products: Tools and equipment for making jewelry

PROSPECTORS POUCH INC
PO Box112
Kennesaw, GA 30144
404-427-6481
Info: Free
Products: Rocks, gemstones, and jewelry making supplies

RAYTECH INDUSTRIES
PO Box 449
Middlefield, CT 06455
203-349-3421
Info: Free
Products: Lapidary equipment

NONFERROUS METALS
PO Box 2595
Waterbury, CT 06723
203-274-7255
Catalog: $3
Products: Brass, copper, bronze, and nickel-silver wire

FLORIDA

HONG KONG LAPIDARY SUPPLIES
2801 University Dr
Coral Springs, FL 33065
305-755-8777
Catalog: $3
Products: Semi-precious gem stones and beads

INTERNATIONAL GEM MERCHANTS INC
4168 Oxford Ave
Jacksonville, FL 32210
904-388-5130
Info: Free
Products: Gemstones

GRAVES COMPANY
1800 Andrews Ave
Pompano Beach
FL 33069
800-327-9103
Catalog: Free
Products: Lapidary equipment

* New listings, NA = Native American, SW = Southwest.

KANSAS

LENTZ LAPIDARY INC
Rt 2 Box 134
Mulvane, KS 67110
316-777-1372
Catalog: $2
Products: Jewelry, mountings, clocks and parts, lapidary equipment

ILLINOIS

* GOLDEN GATE IMPEX INC
917 W Belmont Ave
Chicago, IL 60657 4408
312-9291123
Catalog: $3
Products: Bone/horn pipes, leather cord, beads (bone, glass, metal), and findings

* BEAD WORLD
8 S Brockway St
Palatine, IL 60067-6124
Products: Beads, craft supplies

MASSACHUSETTS

BOSTON FINDINGS AND JEWELERS SUPPLY
387 Washington St 8th Fl
Boston, MA 02108
617-357-9599
Catalog: $2
Products: Jewelry findings and supplies

MICHIGAN

ALETAS ROCK SHOP
1515 Plainfield NE
Grand Rapids, Ml 49505
616-363-5394
Catalog; $1.50
Products: Jewelry-making supplies, tumblers, lapidary equipment, findings, rocks

KINGSLEY NORTH INC
PO Box 216
Norway, Ml 49870
800-338-9280
Catalog: Free
Products: Jewelry-making tools and supplies, lapidary equipment, opals

KERR DIVISION OF SYBRON CORPORATION
PO Box 455
Romulus, Ml 48174
313-946-7800
Catalog: $2
Products: Lapidary equipment, tools, injection wax and molding rubber for making wax patterns

MINNESOTA

MINNESOTA LAPIDARY SUPPLY CORPORATION
2825 Dupont Ave S
Minneapolis, MN 55408
612-872-7211
Catalog: Free
Products: Lapidary equipment

MISSOURI

C & R ENTERPRISES INC
4833 E Park
Springfield, MO 65809
417-866-4843
Catalog: Free
Products: Sterling silver mountings, lapidary supplies, belt buckles, beads, beading supplies, stones

NEVADA

SESCO
PO Box 21406
Reno, NV 89515
800-637-3726
Catalog: Free
Products: Findings, gemstones, fossils, novelties

ANCHOR TOOL AND SUPPLY CO
PO Box 265
Chatham, NJ 07928
201-587-8888
Catalog: $3
Products: Tools and supplies for silversmithing, casting, and blackcasting

H OBODDA AND COMPANY
PO Box 51
Short Hills, NJ 07078
201-467-0212
List: Free
Products: Rare and semi-precious gemstones

NEW MEXICO

* **RIO GRANDE SUPPLY CO**
6901 Washington St NE
Albuquerque
NM 87109-4418
505-345-8511
Catalog: Free
Products: Jewelry making tools, findings, beads, precious metals, gemstones, packaging products

NEW YORK

ALLCRAFT TOOLS AND SUPPLY COMPANY
666 Pacific St
Brooklyn, NY 11207
718-789-2800
Catalog: $5
Products: Lapidary tools and supplies

STARDUST GALLERY
2501 Jericho Tnpk
Centereach, NY 11720
516-981 4302
Catalog: $1
Products: Pearls, crystals, findings and appliques, buttons, studs

DIKRA GEM INC
56 W 45th St Ste 1005
New York, NY 10036
800-873-4572
Info: Free
Products: Semi-precious gem stones

NORTH CAROLINA

ROCK PEDDLER, THE
58 Wedgewood Rd
Franklin, NC 28734
704-524-6042
Catalog: $2
Products: Lapidary equipment

OHIO

CUPBOARD DISTRIBUTING
PO Box 148
Urbana, OH 43078
513-390-6388
Catalog: $2
Products: Wood parts for jewelry making, projects with crafts, toys, woodworking

LAPCRAFT COMPANY INC
195 W Olentangy St
Powell, OH 43065
614-764-8993
Info: Free
Products: Lapidary equipment

CRYSTALITE CORPORATION
18400 Green Meadows Dr N
Westerville, OH 43081
Info: Free
Products: Cabochon machines and lapidary equipment

OREGON

* **CREATOR'S CORNER**
Arts and Crafts
2241 S 6th St
Klamath Falls, OR 97603
Products: Artwork supplies, beads, beading books, classes

RICHARDSONS RECREATIONAL RANCH LTD
Gateway Rt Box 440
Madras, OR 97741
541-475-2680
Info: Free
Products: Rocks, gemstones from worldwide locations; lapidary equipment, clock parts

EDS HOUSE OF GEMS
7712 NE Sandy Blvd
Portland, OR 97211
503-284-8990
Info: Send SASE
Products: Clocks/clockmaking parts, minerals/gems, lapidary equipment, shells, NA relics

PENNSYLVANIA

GILMANS LAPIDARY SUPPLY
PO Box M
Hellertown, PA 18055
215-838-8767
Info: Free
Products: Lapidary equipment, Findings, silver crafting supplies, gemstones

BUCKS COUNTRY CLASSIC
73 Coventry Ln
Lanhorne, PA 19047
800-942-GEMS
Catalog: $2
Products: Freshwater pearls, cabachons, findings, gemstone, handmade, metal, stone beads

T B HAGSTOZ & SON INC
709 Sansom St
Philadelphia, PA 19106
215-922-1627
Catalog: $5
Products: Findings, tools, equipment, solders, silver, bronze, brass-nickel, pewter metals

SOUTH CAROLINA

CARGO HOLD INC
PO Box 239
Charleston, SC 29402
803-723-3341
Catalog: Free
Products: Precious, semi-precious gemstones, sterling silver findings

TEXAS

GOODNOWS
3415 S Hayden St
Amarillo, TX 79109
806-352-0725
List: Free
Products: Gem roughs for faceting, cabbing, tumbling

GEM CENTER USA INC
4100 Alameda Ave
El Paso, TX 79905
915-533-7153
Price list: Free
Products: Geodes and nodules

SWEST INC
11090 N Stemmons Freeway Dallas
TX 75229
214-247-7744
Info: Free
Products: Jewelers tools, wax patterns, findings, gemstones

SOUTHWEST ROCK AND GEM COMPANY
Rt 3 Box 10
Hico, TX 76457
817-796-4907
Price list: Send SASE
Products: Lapidary supplies

VIRGINIA

TRU SQUARE METAL PRODUCTS
PO Box 585
Auburn, VA 98071
800-225-1017
Brochure: Free
Products: Tumblers and other rock polishing equipment

WASHINGTON

BOONE TRADING COMPANY
562 Coyote Rd
Brinnon, WA 98320
206-796-4330
Catalog: $3
Products: Ivory, scrimshaw tusks, Eskimo carvings, fossilized walrus and mammoth ivory tusks/pieces

LORTONE INC
2856 NW Market St
Seattle, WA 98107
206-832-2641
Catalog: Free
Products: Lapidary equipment

WEST VIRGINIA

STONE AGE INDUSTRIES INC
PO Box 383
Powell, WV 82435
307-754-4681
Catalog: $1.50
Products: Rough gemstones, slabs and cutting and polishing equipment, lapidary supplies

WISCONSIN

NASCO
901 Janesville Ave Fort Atkinston, Wl 53538
800-558-9595
Catalog: Free
Products: Jewelry-making supplies and tools

WYOMING

* FT AUGUR TRADING POST
669 W Main St
Lander, WY 82520-3033
307-332-7064
No catalog
Products: Crafting supplies, beads, beadwork, tapes, turquoise/silver jewelry, antlers, leather, skulls

* New listings, NA = Native American,
SW = Southwest.

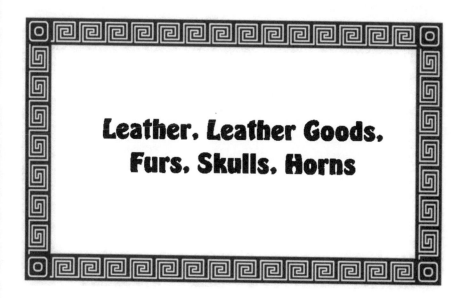

Leather, Leather Goods, Furs, Skulls, Horns

ALASKA

* KODIAK FURS
425 D St
Anchorage
AK 99501-2325
Products: Alaskan furs,
more

ARIZONA

*** LIVING NATURE
CREATIONS**
PO Box 3694
Sedona, AZ 86340
800-430-7988
Brochure: Free
Products: Moccasins:
buffalo hide, custom
made for exact fit;
fringes and sheepskin
lining optional

ARKANSAS

*** BUFFALO TRADE
COMPANY**
D-J Enterprises
PO Box 898
Mountain View
AR 72560
501-269-2445
Products: Custom
leather work, equipment
for archers, muzzle
loading supplies, books,
gifts

IOWA

SMOOTH STONE
604 Worth
Ackley, IA 50601
515-847-2552
Products: Hand-
worked brain tan deer
skins

KANSAS

*** BLANKETS & SPOTS
LEATHER STORE**
2249 27th Road NE
Waverly, KS 66871
Products: Leather
goods

MONTANA

*** GREAT
NORTHWEST FUR
AND TRADING POST**
PO Box 88
Heron, MT 59844-0088
Products: Furs, trade
goods

TEXAS

HIGH SIERRA FURS
414 Scarlett
Baytown, TX 77520
800-594-8266
Brochure: Free
Products: Steerhides,
lambskin, alpacas,
exotics, 100s of hides

WISCONSIN

*** BISONRIDGE
LEATHER**
PO Box 72
Packwaukee, WI 53953
608-589-5500
Brochure: Free
Products: Coats, hats,
purses, medicine bags,
decorator items, from
bison fur and leather

---

* New listings, NA = Native American,
SW = Southwest.

Native American and Southwestern Clothing

GENERAL LISTING

BETTY DAVID
206-726-2110
Catalog: Available
Products: NA custom coats, hand-painted lamb shearling

ALASKA

* MUSK OX PRODUCERS COOP
604 H St
Anchorage
AK 99501-3415
Info: Send SASE
Products: Hand-knitted Qiviut scarves, caps, tunics, other clothing

ARIZONA

WESTWIND ORIGINALS
8711 E Pinnacle Peak Rd #111
Scottsdale, AZ 85255
800-484-9560
Brochure: Call
Products: T-shirts, shorts, night shirts, sweatshirts, with western and NA designs, handpainted

UWIGA DESIGNS
3420 E Maxim Pl
Tucson, AZ 85739
520-825-2830
Catalog: $6
Products: Shirt jackets and other western clothing with handpainted pockets, NA designs

COLORADO

TRIBAL DESIGNS
PO Box 341
Crestone, CO 81131
719-256-4455
Products: Custom made handbags made with deer/elk hide, silver conchos, wool, Zapotec weavings

MILLER STOCKMAN
Western Wear
PO Box 5127
Denver, CO 80217-5127
800-688-9888
Products: Western wear, shirts, boots, hats, accessories, more

APPALOOSA TRADING CO
501 Main Ave
Durango, CO 81301
907-259-1994
Products: Handcrafted leather belts, tooled belt buckles, sterling bolos, badges, concho belts, more

CONNECTICUT

TRIBAL WEAR BY SKINZ
27 Summit Rd
Riverside, CT 06878
203-637-7884
Products: NA clothing; specializes in reproductions of old war shirts; caters to galleries, museums

GEORGIA

WESTERN HEART
372 Powderhorn
St Marys, GA 31558
912-882-8976
Catalog: $3
Products: Western shirts and accessories

MONTANA

SCHNEES BOOTS & SHOES
6597 Falcon Ln
Bozeman, MT 59715
800-922-1562
Products: "Arrow Moccasin Company" brand contemporary hand-sewn heavy moccasins

* New listings, NA = Native American, SW = Southwest.

* NORTHERN PLAINS INDIAN CRAFTS ASSOCIATION
PO Box E
Browning
MT 59417-3006
406-338-5661
Price list: Send SASE
Products: Buckskin vests, gloves, handbags, moccasins, beadwork, jewelry, belts, dolls, regalia

* ALL SORTS INC
PO Box 975
Wolf Point
MT 59201-0975
406-653-3011
Products: Embroidery, caps, jackets, totes, briefcases, and many others

NEBRASKA

SANDHILLS TACK
221 N Main St
Gordon, NE 69343
308-282-2944
Products: Western and SW gifts, and western boots and quality tack

NEW YORK

* GOOD MEDICINE WAY, THE
116 Seaman Ave #3E
New York
NY 10034-2875
Flyer: Free
Products: Trader, specializes in traditional ribbon shirts, Cherokee tier dresses and skirts

NORTH CAROLINA

* TUSCARORA INDIAN HANDCRAFT SHOP
RR 4 Box172
Maxton, NC 28364-9517
910-844-3352
Price list: Send SASE
Products: Moccasins, shirts, hats, vests, handbags, pouches, head bands, belts, necklaces, jewelry

OKLAHOMA

CHA' TULLIS DESIGNS
108 W Main St
Hominy, OK 74035
918-885-4717
Catalog: $5
Products: T-shirts, pillows, and potholders with NA themes

* BUFFALO SUN
PO Box 1556
Miami, OK 74355-1556
918-542-8879
Info: Send SASE
Products: Traditional and contemporary NA blouses, skirts, ribbon shirts, dresses, jackets, coats, etc

* MONKAPEME
PO Box 457
Perkins, OK 74059-0457
405-547-2948
Info: Send SASE
Products: NA contemporary fashions, traditional costumes, moccasins, dresses, shirts

OREGON

DEUCES WILD DESIGNS
PO Box 17894
Salem, OR 97305
Products: Sweatshirts with painted horse or galloping buffalo design

SOUTH DAKOTA

PLAINS, THE
PO Box 380
Eagle Butte, SD 57625
605-964-4610
Products: Western and casual wear, boots, T-shirts, beading supplies

79

* JACKSON ORIGINALS

PO Box 1049
Mission, SD 57555-1049
605-856-2541
Catalog: $1
Products: Handmade
contemporary buckskin
jackets, vests, dresses,
skirts, NA/western
motifs

* CONTEMPORARY LAKOTA FASHION

235 Curtis St Apt 12
Rapid City
SD 57701-0668
605-341-7560
Info: Send SASE
Products: Ribbon shirts,
skirts, dresses, shawls,
vests, star quilts

TEXAS

DOUBLE L LEATHERWORKS

PO Box 1271
Taylor, TX 76574
512-352-6640
Catalog: $1
Products: Leather shop-
ping totes, wallets, bags,
overnighters, satchels,
hand-tooled

WISCONSIN

W C RUSSELL MOCCASIN CO

285 SW Franklin
Berlin, Wl 54923-0309
414-361-2252
Catalog: Free
Products:
Contemporary "moc-
casin" shoes

---

* New listings, NA = Native American,
SW = Southwest.

Southwest Furniture, Woodwork

ALABAMA

ROYAL HOUSE, THE
2410 Fairway Dr
Mountain Brook
AL 35213
205-879-0888
Products: Handcarved, solid rose wood antique reproduction furniture

ARIZONA

SIMPLY SOUTHWESTERN
5441 W Hadley St
Phoenix, AZ 85043
620-278-8054
Products: Antique distressed doors of Old Tucson series, to rustic, hand-forged door hardware

BILL HUBARTT
PO Box 36596
Tucson, AZ 85740
520-297-8010
Products: Craftsman of SW door designing and architectural work

EQUIPAL FURNITURE
Jungle Zoo
PO Box 809
Tucson, AZ 85702
520-99-JUNGLE
Catalog: $3
Products: SW-flavor handcrafted furniture, rosewood/cedar/palma frames/pigskin

ARKANSAS

C WALKER AND COMPANY
1002 Gay St
Corning, AR 72422
800-853-5030
Brochure: $5
Products: Handmade, handpainted wall and medicine cabinets, and shelves; other items

WOODS BY WILD BILL
471 Polk 67
Mena, AR 71953
501-394-4184
Products: Wildlife and western carving on home furnishings

BANTA WOOD PRODUCTS
HC 67 Box 16 A
Ogden, AR 71961
501-326-4833
Products: Oak or Arkansas pine home accessories, quilt shelves, peg shelves

CALIFORNIA

CREATIONS FROM THE SEA WOOD SALVAGE STUDIO
229 Tewksburgy Ave Pt
Richmond by the Bay
CA 94801
510-233-9663
Brochure: Available
Products: Adirondack style furniture handmade from wine barrels and salvaged wood from barns

VROOMAN WOODCARVINGS
PO Box 2883
Truckee, CA 96160
916-587-8104
Products: Handcarved, handpainted quail and cactus lamp, of lodge pole pine; parchment shade

COLORADO

SHAGGY RAM, THE
PO Box 2378
Avon, CO 81620
970-949-4377
Products: Antique country furniture

* New listings, NA = Native American,
SW = Southwest.

NORMERICA
CUSTOM COUNTRY
HOMES
**Smith & Smith
Enterprises**
40 Sunset Dr Ste 10
Basalt, CO 81621
970-927-4755
Brochure and video:
Available
Products: Post and
beam country home
design

KNUDSEN GLOSS
1820 Riverbend Rd
Boulder, CO 30301
303-112-5882
Products: Architects
and planners, mountain
homes

MADEIRAS
30th and Walnut
Boulder, CO
303-443-3078
Products: Antique
reproductions and clas-
sic furniture for rustic
living

QUIET MOOSE, THE
326 S Main
Breckenridge, CO
800-303-6151
Catalog: Available
Products: Mountain
rustic, lodge, cottage,
and antique home fur-
nishings and accessories

**SNOWMASS LOG
FURNITURE**
1107 Hendricks Blvd
Carbondale, CO 81623
303-963-9099
Products: Log furniture,
antler lamps, chande-
liers, mirrors

**STUART BUCHANAN
ANTIQUES**
1530 15th St
Denver, CO 80202
303-825-1222
Products: Antique
country furnishings

**BRISTLCONE PINE
COMPANY**
5775 E Best Road
Larkspur, CO 80118
303-688-0557
Video: $7.59
Products: Natural
bristlecone pine furnish-
ings

**KITCHEN
DISTRIBUTORS INC**
1309 W Littleton Blvd
Littleton, CO
303-795-0665
Products: Country/
western wood cabinetry

**PAYNE FURNITURE
GALLERY**
538 Village #4150
Pagosa Springs
CO 81147
970-731-4022
Products: SW furniture
with western and NA
handcarved designs

NORMERICA
CUSTOM COUNTRY
HOMES
Elk River Realty
811 Lincoln Ave
Steamboat Springs
CO 80977
970-879-8103
Brochure, video:
Available
Products: Post and
beam country home
design

CONNECTICUT

GATES MOORE
11 River Rd Silvermine
Norwalk, CT 06850
203-847-3231
Catalog: $2
Products: Wooden
chandeliers, copper
lanterns and wall
sconces

**LUMINARIOS
STUDIOS**
PO Box 253
Stony Creek, CT 06405
203-483-7068
Catalog: $9
Products: Sculptural
handcrafted pole fur-
nishings, with deerhide
and Native weaving

GEORGIA

**EDDY WEST
COLLECTION OF
HAMPTON ALL**
PO Box 786
Clarkesville, GA 30523
800-829-9037
Catalog: $5
Products: Solid pine
furniture line, handcraft-
ed by North Georgia
artisans

**APPALACHIAN
RUSTIC
FURNISHINGS**
PO Box 263
Rising Fawn, GA 30738
706-462-2447
Products: Appalachian-
touch hickory chairs,
handmade in the north
Georgia mountains

INDIANA

**WOODSTOCK
FURNITURE CO**
PO Box 2401
Elkhart, IN 46515
219-294-2782
Products: Handcrafted,
hand painted home fur-
niture

HERBES AND TWIGS
PO Box 1081
Nashville, IN 47448
812-837-9515
Catalog: $5
Products: Rustic home
furnishings, custom-
crafted pieces suitable
from Adirondacks to
high Sierras

**ROUDEBUSH CO,
THE**
Box 348
Star City, IN 46985
800-847-4947
Products: Handcrafted
oak furniture (personal-
ization available)

KANSAS

**BUILDING BLOCK,
THE**
PO Box 522
Fredonia, KS 66736
800-439-2634
Info: Call
Products: Cedar-lined
solid pine trunks, fin-
ished or unfinished; deal-
er inquiries welcomed

LOUISIANA

SAVANNAS
9510 Linwood Ave
Shreveport, LA 71106
318-688-5298
Layaways available
Products: Hand crafted
and painted by
Louisiana folk artists:
Heirloom quality wood-
en furniture

MARYLAND

**DISTINCTIVE WOOD
DESIGNS**
28 S Potomac St
Hagerstown, MD 21740
301-714-1608
Products: Solid oak and
cherry furniture with
antique finish

MICHIGAN

PRESTIGE IN WOOD
1847 Parr Hwy
Adrian, MI 49221
517-263-4238
Catalog: $2
Products: Children's
wooden furnishings and
toys

---

* New listings, NA = Native American,
SW = Southwest.

PFEIFFER CUSTOM FURNISHINGS INC
3138 Farmbrook Ln
Metamora, Ml 48455
810-482-0895
Products: SW-style handcrafted wooden bedroom sets

PINEWOOD STUDIOS
4829 Mac Arthur
Muskegon, Ml 49442
616-777-3889
Products: Rustic weathered home Furnishings of pine slabs

MISSISSIPPI

NOSTALGIA HANDCRAFTED FURNITURE INC
5114 Hwy 182 E
Columbus, MS 39702
601-328-7310
Products: Handcarved home furnishings

MONTANA

LODGECRAFT BY MONTANA WOOD DESIGNS
PO Box 1303
Eureka, MT 59917
406-296-2547
Video catalog: $10
Products: Rustic lodge-look natural style furnishings, 20+ piece product line

NEVADA

LIZARD HISS STUDIO
PO Box 20542
Sun Valley, NV 89433
702-673-6278
Products: Rug holder for wall display of heavy textiles, made of clear pine

NEW MEXICO

ARETSANOS IMPORTS CO
PO Drawer G
Santa Fe, NM 87504
505-983-1743
Catalog: Call
Products: Whitewash equipal furniture, handmade

LA PUERTA
1302 Cerrillos Rd
Santa Fe, NM 87505
800-984-8164
Products: Antique and Spanish colonial doors Large collection

MORRELLI CORPORATION
540 S Guadalupe
Santa Fe, NM 87501
800-739-6886
Products: Craftsman of SW doors and furniture

SPANISH PUEBLO DOORS
1091 Siler Rd Unit B1
Santa Fe, NM 87501
505-473-0464
Catalog: Free
Products: Native New Mexican and custom doors in Santa Fe style

NEW YORK

BARRY GREGSONS ADIRONDACK RUSTICS GALLERY
Charley Hill Rd
Schroon Lake, NY 12870
518-932-9384
Brochure/price list: $1
Products: Rocking chairs featuring curly maple, cherry, yellow birch; settees, chairs, tables available

NORTH CAROLINA

TRADITIONAL CHAIRS BY CANDLERTOWN
PO Box 1630
Candler, NC 28715
704-667-4844
Brochure: $2
Products: High Country wood furniture, in cherry, walnut, oak, and maple

NORMANS HANDMADE REPRODUCTIONS
Rt 6 Box 695
Dunn, NC 28334
910-892-4349
Brochure/price list: $3
Products: Solid mahogany hand crafted beds; available also in cherry or pine

CREATIONS BY CRANFORD
PO Box 9007
Hickory, NC 28603
704-326-9707
Brochure: $2
Products: Furniture pieces in honey pine, white, or blue finishes

* ROBERT D WAYNEE SR
PO Box 5232
New Bern, NC 28560
919-637-2546
Info: Send SASE
Products: NA wood sculptures

BARNES AND BARNES FURNITURE
190 Commerce Ave
Southern Pines
NC 28387
800-334-8174
Products: Shaker style home furnishings

BLACKWELDERS OF NORTH CAROLINA
294 Turnersburg Hwy
Statesville, NC 28677
800-438-0201
Catalog: Available
Products: Furniture crafted from antique weathered pine in aged whitewash or honey pine finish

OHIO

AMERICAN WOOD AND IRON
1227 Borden Ave SW
Massillon, OH 44647
216-833-8149
Products: Oak and iron home furnishings, western style

OKLAHOMA

* JACK GREGORY
RR 1 Box 79
Watts, OK 74964-9701
918-723-5408
Info: Send SASE
Products: Contemporary handmade wood candle holders, bowls, lamps and jewelry, plates, more

PENNSYLVANIA

MENALLEN ROAD JOINERY
511 W King St
East Berlin, PA 17316
717-259-7502
Brochure: $2
Products: 18th and 19th century Pennsylvania folk art accessories and collectibles; dower chests

CEDAR CREEK COB
PO Box 71
Lowber, PA 15660
412-446-1620
Catalog: $2
Products: Wood country home accessories

PBJ INTERNATIONAL
PO Box 373
Mountville, PA 17554
717-291-5936
Catalog: Free
Products: Solid oak furnishings by an Amish furniture maker

CARSONS COUNTRY STEW
245 Grist Mill Rd
New Holland, PA 17557
717-354-7343
Catalog: $5
Products: Hand-painted furniture made from timeworn barn boards, shutters and hardware

* New listings, NA = Native American, SW = Southwest.

GENESEE RIVER TRADING CO
PO Box 126
New Wilmington
PA 16142
412-533-5354
Products: Oak bentwood rockers, handcrafted by Old Order Amish

CONKLINS RD
1 Box 70
Susquehanna, PA 18847
717-465-3832
Products: Antique barnwood and hand hewn beams

AGED WOODS
2331 E Market St
York PA 17402
800-233-9307
Brochure: Free
Products: Antique wide plank flooring for homes; barnwood, oak, chestnut, other woods

DUTCH CRAFTER, THE
728 Hemlock Square
Zelienople, PA 16063
412-452-1321
Products: Antique replica Amish rocking chairs, built of oak and barked hickory saplings

PARKER BROOKS FURNITURE MAKERS
PO Box 638
Saylorsburg, PA 18353
717-424-9481
Products: Rustic wood furniture; handcrafted pine

TENNESSEE

QUALITY CRAFTING
PO Box 3181
Morristown
TN 37815-3181
423-586-8236
Products: Wooden furniture

SEALS FURNITURE CO
303 Simpson Rd
Whitesburg, TN 37891
423-235-3200
Products: Oak and walnut home furnishings

TEXAS

HEARTLAND GENERAL STORE
1251 W Magnolia St
Fort Worth, TX 76104
800-856-8060
Products: Oak mirrors, stands, armoires, tables, beds, treasure chests; rustic Mexican colonial

TRUNKLINE
111 S Colket St
Kerens, TX 75144
903-396-7254
Products: Wooden end tables and trunks

WOOD CREATIONS
PO Box 4085
Tyler, TX 75712
800-586-5803
Brochure: Free
Products: Barnwood-framed western prints

UTAH

OLD WORLD CARVING
728 Aspen Ln
Park City, UT 84060
801-649-7877
Products: Maple handcarved home furnishings; western and wildlife carvings

BROTHERS BROTHERS
590 S 400 W
Provo, UT 84601
801-373-7588
Catalog: $3
Products: Mountain Pine Collection home furnishings

TIMBERLINE MANUFACTURING
3044 S 300 E
Salt Lake City, UT 84115
801-466-1485
Products: Pine home furnishings

UTAH MOUNTAIN LOG
1626 S 700 W
Salt Lake City, UT 84104
801-977-1188
Info: Call
Products: Lodgepole furniture, rustic to contemporary

ASPEN SPRING CREATIONS
9005 S 3605 E
Sandy, UT 84093
800-750-4761
Portfolio: $5
Products: Wood home accessories

VIRGINIA

LARKS REPRODUCTION FURNITURE
704 Seymour Dr South
Boston, VA 24592
804-572-3211
Products: Hand-crafted walnut and mahogany furniture, gun cabinets and other woodwork

WYOMING

HIGH COUNTRY ACCENTS
PO Box AE
Jackson, WY 83001
307-734-1301
Ship anywhere
Products: Western wood and leather home furnishings

ROCKY MOUNTAIN LODGEPOLE
N Main Evanston
WY 82931
307-789-9042
Brochure: Call
Products: Lodgepole log and rustic furniture; custom work available

* New listings, NA = Native American, SW = Southwest.

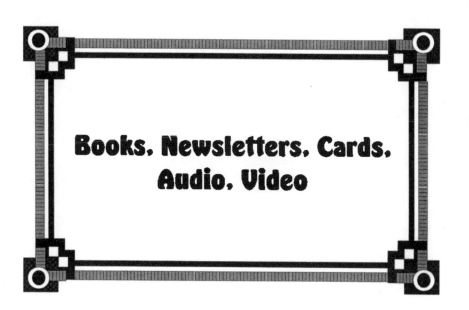

Books, Newsletters, Cards,
Audio, Video

GENERAL LISTINGS

BOOKS BEYOND BORDERS
800-347-6440
Products: NA books

BLUE DOLPHIN PUBLISHING
800-643-0765
Products: NA books

COUNTRY COLLECTIONS
800-856-8060
Products: Magazine of traditional, French, Country, Shaker, and Lodge and Primitive furnishings

INDIAN MARKET MAGAZINE
800-757-5278
Subscriptions
Products: Guide to the Santa Fe Indian Market; history, booth info, Indian arts programs, more

JOHN MUIR PUBLISHING
800-888-7504
Products: NA books

MUSEUM OF NEW MEXICO PRESS
505-827-0654
Products: NA books

PRUETT PUBLISHING
303-449-4919
Products: Southwestern and Spanish recipe cookbooks, other SW/western books

RED CRANE BOOKS
800-922-3392
Products: Large selection of NA books

THREE STARS COMPUTER SERVICES
541-942-6144
Products: Personalized childrens books, calendars, coloring books, puzzles

ZANGO MUSIC
800-688-0187
Wholesale only, info is free
Products: NA music, catalog has 40 pgs, 400 titles

ARIZONA

CANYONLANDS PUBLICATIONS AND INDIAN ARTS
PO Box 16175
Bellemont
AZ 86015-6175
Products: NA books, Indian items

COOL RUNNINGS
PO Box 3564
Window Rock
AZ 86515-3564
520-871-5600
Catalog: Available
Products: NA music, cassettes/CDs and videos, moccasins, arts and crafts, Retail/wholesale.

INSTITUTE FOR TRIBAL ENVIRONMENTAL PROFS
Northern Arizona University
520-523-9555
Products: Publishes a national directory of tribal environmental programs

NORTHLAND PUBLISHING
Flagstaff, AZ
Products: NA books

---

* New listings, NA = Native American, SW = Southwest.

**SOUTHWEST
MARKETING**
PO Box 18244
Fountain Hills
AZ 85269
602-837-4282
Products: NA 24-month
calendars

ARKANSAS

*** AMERICAN NATIVE
PRESS ARCHIVES**
University of Arkansas
502 Stabler Hall
2801 S University Ave
Little Rock, AR 72204
Products: Native writings

CALIFORNIA

**HAPPY TRAILS
Childrens Foundation**
PO Box 1647
Apple Valley, CA 92307
Products: Nat'l Festival
of the West posters;
assists children's foundation

*** NATIONAL MAIL
ORDER GUIDE**
19579 Temescal Canyon
Rd #1044
Corona, CA 91719-5658
Products: Guide carries
Indian related sources

**PACIFIC WESTERN
TRADERS**
305 Wool St
Folsom CA 95630-2550
916-985-3851
Products: NA books
Trade shows, NA merchandise, beading supplies, carvings, drums,
more

**CROSSING PRESS,
THE**
PO Box 1048
Freedom, CA 95019
408-722-0711
Products: NA books,
postcards, calendars,
journals

**ANNDELS COUNTRY
TOUCH GREETINGS**
PO Box 0910
Garden Grove
CA 92642-0916
714-537-1659
Products: Western style
calendars, greeting cards

**BEAD DIRECTORY,
THE**
PO Box 10103
Oakland, CA 94610
510-452-0836 Call for
info
Products: Publication,
"The Bead Directory,"
listing sources for beads
and bead supplies

AUDIO LITERATURE
370 W San Bruno
San Bruno, CA 94066
800-383-0174
Catalog: Free
Products: NA literary
cassettes; titles include
Russell Means, and
Black Elk titles

*** INDIAN
HISTORIAN PRESS**
1493 Masonic Ave
San Francisco
CA 94117-4525
Products: Indian literature

COLORADO

**CREEKSIDE BOOKS
AND ART**
PO Box 1234
Buena Vista, CO 81211
719-395-6416
Catalog: None
Products: "The best
selection of NA titles in
central Colorado" (NA
books)

* HOW 2 BOOKS
Box 5793
Denver, CO 80217
800-284-8218
Brochure: Free
Products: NA how-to
books about beadwork,
earrings, jewelry, pins,
millefiori, other beaded
items

WICONI WASTE
PO Box 480005
Denver, CO 80248
303-238-3420
Products: Non-profit corporation for cross-cultural understanding, books, recordings, merchandise

MULTI CULTURE PUBLISHING
636 N Taft Hill Rd
Fort Collins, CO 80521
Products: NA books

* RIF RAF RECORDS
PO Box 413
Salida, CO 81201-0413
719-539-5457
Products: NA recordings

FLORIDA

GEORGE A ROBERTS
PO Box 1293
Ocala, FL 34478
Products: A book about NA flags, emblems, symbols, etc

GEORGIA

* POWWOW A LIVING TRADITION
842-B N Highland Ave
Atlanta, GA 30306-4530
404-874-1620
Flyer: Free
Poster: $5 wholesale
Products: NA trading cards, 100 images of living Indian dancers, singers, children, elders, etc

LOUISIANA

WHISPERING WIND MAGAZINE
PO Box 1390
Folsom, LA 70437-1390
800-301-8009
Products: Magazine presenting NA craft info, articles, culture, etc

MAINE

COUNTRY ROADS PRESS
PO Box 286
Castine, ME 04421
Products: SW and western guides

MARYLAND

NATIVE EXPERIENCE, THE
7406 Waldran Ave
Temple Hills, MD 20748
301 449-6730
Products: NA publishers; seeking NA / African American individuals for inclusion in book, "Black Indians"

MASSACHUSETTS

HOBOMOCK HOMESITE
Plimouth Plantation
PO Box 1620
Plymouth, MA
508-746-1622
Products: NA art calendars, crafts

MISSOURI

CRC PUBLISHING COMPANY
PO Box 22583
Kansas City
MO 64113-0583
816-361-2059
Brochure: Free
Products: Multicultural grant guides

---

* New listings, NA = Native American,
SW = Southwest.

MICHIGAN

EARLY AMERICAN ARTISTRY
Drawer 99
West Olive, Ml 49460
Products: Book about tomahawks, pipe axes of the American frontier

NEW JERSEY

SCRIBNER SIMON & SCHUSTER
200 Old Tappan Rd
Old Tappan, NJ 07675
800-223-2336
Products: NA books

NEW MEXICO

* TEMPLE OF THE SPIRIT
PO Box 9132
Albuquerque
NM 87119-9132
505-873-2179
Catalog: Free
Products: Silk-screened greeting cards, art prints featuring rock art and spirit visions

INDIAN TRADER
PO Box 1421
Gallup, NM 87305-1421
505-722-6694
Subscription
Products: NA monthly newspaper, info on NA arts, crafts, cultures, history, book reviews, more

PAN-AMERICAN INDIAN ASSN
PO Box 58
Montezuma
NM 87731-0058
505-454-9413
Catalog: Free
Newspaper: $1
Products: "Earthkeeper" quarterly tabloid newspaper

* MULTI CULTURE PUBLISHING
2442 Cerrillos Rd Ste 367
Santa Fe
NM 87505-3262
Products: NA books

NEW YORK

AMERICAN INDIAN PROGRAM
Cornell University
PO Box DH
Ithaca, NY 14851-9963
Products: Publications, books, magazines

GREENFIELD REVIEW PRESS
PO Box 308
Greenfield Center
NY 12833
518-583-1440
Products: NA books

WILLIAM MORROW AND CO
1350 Avenue of the Americas
New York, NY 10019
Products: SW cookbooks, other western/SW/NA books

NORTH CAROLINA

MALAPROPS BOOKSTORE
61 Haywood St
Asheville, NC 28801
Products: NA books

* MUSIC OF THE WORLD
PO Box 3620
Chapel Hill
NC 27515-3620
919-932-9600
Catalog: Free
Products: Trad and contemp music from around the world, incl NA music from SW, S Plains

NORTH DAKOTA

UNITED TRIBES TECHNICAL COLLEGE
Arrow Graphics
3315 University Dr
Bismarck, ND 58504
701-255-3285 ext 293
Products: Indian recipe book

93

OKLAHOMA

**UNIVERSITY OF
OKLAHOMA PRESS**
1005 Asp Ave
Norman, OK 73019
800-627-7377
Catalog: Free
Products: NA books

**FULL CIRCLE
COMMUNICATIONS**
1131 S College Ave
Tulsa, OK 74104-4120
800-940-8849
Brochure: Free
Products: NA how-to
videos, about beadwork,
dancing, baskets, shell-
work, ribbonwork,
clothing etc

RED VINYL RECORDS
8086 S Yale Ste 146
Tulsa, OK 74136
Products: NA CDs, cas-
settes, T-shirts

OREGON

COMMON CRAFTS
PO Box 5012
Central Point
OR 97502-0042
541-664-1651
Flyer: Free
Products: Arrowhead
making video and
books, arrowhead mak-
ing supplies

**SPOTTED HORSE
TRIBAL GIFTS**
PO Box 869
Oakridge
OR 97463-0869
Catalog: $2
Products: Native
American directory;
Cherokee research/books
guide; other NA books,
goods

*** SPILYAY TYMOO
Tribes of Warm Springs**
PO Box 870
Warm Springs
OR 97761-0870
541-553-3274
Subscription: $9 year
Products: Newspaper
published bi weekly, lat-
est Indian-related and
local news

PENNSYLVANIA

LAPIDARY JOURNAL
PO Box 124
Devon, PA 19333-0124
Products: Magazine for
the lapidary and jewel-
ry-making industries

**MAUROSE
PUBLISHING CO**
PO Box 2153
Moscow, PA 18444
800-391-0011
Products: NA books

SOUTH DAKOTA

DOUBLE M STUDIOS
Box 741
Pine Ridge, SD 57770
605-867-5993
Products: Native
American calendars,
retail/wholesale

BOBBY EAGLE
Box 403
Waubay, SD 57273
605-947-4901
Products: NA record-
ings

**BOOK AND
COMPANY**
Rapid City, SD
800-640-6164
Products: NA books

OYATE RECORDS
3907 Minnekahta
Rapid City, SD 57702
800-471-0637 ext 0973
Products: NA music
recordings

TENNESSEE

**BOOK PUBLISHING
COMPANY**
PO Box 99
Summertown
TN 384483
800-695-2241
Catalog: Free
Products: NA books by
NA authors

* New listings, NA = Native American,
SW = Southwest.

**SPIRIT KEEPER, THE
E TN**
Indian League Inc
PO Box 6253
Knoxville, TN 37914
Newsletter: Write
Products: Membership
in ETIL, and newsletter

TEXAS

*** A TRIBE OF TWO
PRESS**
PO Box 913 Georgetown
TX 78627-0913
Products: NA publica-
tions

UTAH

**GIBBS SMITH
PUBLISHER**
PO Box 667
Layton, UT 84041
Products: Western
books, books about log
homes, more

WASHINGTON

**HANCOCK HOUSE
PUBLISHERS**
1431 Harrison Ave
Blaine, WA 98230
800-938-1114
Catalog: Free
Products: NA books

WISCONSIN

NORTHWARD PRESS
Minocqua, Wl
800-336-5666
Products: NA books

CANADA

**BEAR CLAN
RECORDS**
10520 Yonge St Unit 35B
Ste 144
Richmond Hill, Ontario
Canada L4C 3C7
905-884-0179
Products: NA record-
ings

*** NATIVE BOOK
CENTRE**
**North Am Indian
Books**
150 York Hill Blvd
Thornhill
Ontario UJ 2P6
Canada
905-881-7804
Catalog: Free
Products: Books about
Native Americans

Food, Seeds, Herbs, Botanicals

CALIFORNIA

* WALK IN BEAUTY
PO Box 1331
Colfax, CA 95713
916-346-7143
Catalog/class calendar: $1
Products: Organic
herbs, supplies, essential
oils, books, herbal gifts,
classes, newsletter

COLORADO

*** MEDICINE ROOT,
INC**
PO Box 788
Louisville, CO 80027
303-665-3476
Products: NA food gift
baskets, buffalo meat
products, herbs, seeds,
beadwork, quillwork,
more

*** HERB COMPANION,
THE**
Interweave Press
201 E 4th St Dept K-DC
Loveland
CO 80537-9977
800-645-3675
Products: Magazine on
the use and cultivation,
etc, of herbals

ILLINOIS

*** INTERNATIONAL
HERB ASSN**
1202 Allanson Rd
Mundelein
IL 60060-3808
Products: Native herb
info

MARYLAND

*** HOT SAUCE CLUB
OF AMERICA**
PO Box 5784
Baltimore
MD 21208-0784
Products: Club for hot
sauce enthusiasts

MINNESOTA

*** MANITOK FOODS &
GIFTS, KENOO FINE
CRAFTS**
PO Box 97 Callaway
MN 56521-0097
800-726-1863
Catalog/brochure: Free
Products: Hand har-
vested wild rice, wild
berry jellies, birch bark
crafts jewelry, dolls,
quilts, gift baskets

MISSOURI

*** EVENING SHADE
FARMS**
RR 2 Box 281
Osceola, MO 64776
417-282-6985
Catalog: Available
Products: Natural
herbal soaps, body
products

MONTANA

GUNSMOKE
USPO General Delivery
Red Lodge, MT 59068
Products: Bar-b-cue
foods, cowboy gift sets,
sauces, chili mixin's,
spice rubs

NORTH CAROLINA

*** WEETOCK
TOBACCO**
PO Box 1282
Swansboro, NC 28584
800-548-3870
Info: Free
Products: Info, growing
your own tobacco legally

OKLAHOMA

* CHEROKEE LADY
HC 37 Box 10
Locust Grove, OK 74352
Products: Indian herbs
and plants

* New listings, NA = Native American,
SW = Southwest.

OREGON

**SILETZ TRIBAL
SMOKEHOUSE**
PO Box 1004
Depoe Bay, OR 97341
541-765-2286/800-828-4269
Flyer: Free
Products: Smoked
salmon, jerky, lox, bead-
work, gift boxes, tapes
Indian-owned enter

WASHINGTON

*** HEALTHY THISTLE
BOTANICALS
Culinary & Medicinal
Herbs**
PO Box 745
Poulsbo, WA 98370
360-697-1868
Catalog: $1
Products: Culinary and
medicinal herbs by mail
prise

---

* New listings, NA = Native American,
SW = Southwest.

Native American Organizations, Services, and Miscellaneous

GENERAL LISTINGS

AMERICAN INDIAN ART MARKET
CA
408-659-5205
Products:
Contemporary and traditional work by 50 NA artists

ART OF THE AMERICAN INDIAN FRONTIER
http//www/glrain/glrain
Products: Produces Native cultural, historical, language materials on the Internet

ARTISTS FOR AMERICAN INDIANS
http://www.dgsys.com/—aihf/index.html
Products: Project of Am Ind Heritage Found Museum-like exhibitions in cyberspace

CANYON COUNTRY ORIGINALS
http://www.canyonart.com
Products: Internet site featuring NA pottery, art, gallery items

FOND DU LAC COMMUNITY COLLEGE
218-879-0800
Products: NA community college

NATIONAL INDIAN GAMING ASSN
202-546-7711
Products: Conferences, seminars, golf tournaments, awards banquets conventions, trade shows

NATIVE AMERICAN TELEVISION
612-825-9525
Products: Film series documents inside look at Native people and at issues in Indian Country

OLD WEST AND TRIBAL ART SHOW AND SALE
Sharon Good
602-596-8985
Products: Antique and contemporary NA and tribal art shows

WESTERN LIFESTYLE EXPO
303-355-1402
Products: Western celebration; art, entertainment, NA arts and crafts, dance, music, fashions, more

ALABAMA

* ALABAMA INDIAN AFFAIRS COMMISSION
669 S Lawrence St
Montgomery
AL 36104-5849
Products: NA Indian Affairs bureau

ALASKA

* ALASKA WILDLIFE ALLIANCE, THE
PO Box 202022
Anchorage
AK 99520-2022
Products: Wildlife organization in Alaska

* KOAHNIC BROADCAST CORP
810 E 9th Ave
Anchorage
AK 99501-3826
Products: Native radio station

COUNCIL OF ATHABASCAN TRIBAL GOVERNMENTS
PO Box 33
Fort Yukon, AK
Products: Alaskan Native organization

* New listings, NA = Native American, SW = Southwest.

ALASKA REGIONAL HEALTH CONSORTIUM
222 Tongass Dr
Sitka, AK 99835
907-966-2451
Products: Village-based health care providers

ARIZONA

COCONO CENTER FOR THE ARTS
2300 N Fort Valley Rd
Flagstaff, AZ 86001
520-779-6921
Festival of NA arts
Products: Juried exhibits, outdoor markets, Call to NA artists to participate

* ZION NATIONAL HISTORY ASSN SHOP
HC 65 Box 5
Fredonia, AZ 86022
520-443-7329
Products: NA cultural and historical information source

AK-CHIN-DAK MUSEUM
PO Box 897
Maricopa, AZ 85239
520-568-9487
Products: NA exhibits

* COLORADO RIVER INDIAN TRIBAL MUSEUM
RR Z Box 23-B
Parker, AZ 85344-9704
520-669-9211 ext 336
Products: NA exhibits

SAN CARLOS APACHE CULTURAL CENTER
PO Box 760
Peridot, AZ 85542
520-475-2394
Products: NA arts and crafts

* ARIZONA COMMISSION ON INDIAN AFFAIRS
1645 W Jefferson St
Ste 127
Phoenix, AZ 85007-3004
Products: NA bureau

ATLATLE
2303 N Central Ave
Ste 104
Phoenix, AZ 85004
602-253-2731
Products: Nat'l service org for NA arts, Networking, presenting NA art, training, leadership developing

* HEARD MUSEUM, THE
22 E Monte Vista Rd
Phoenix, AZ 85004-1433
602-252-8840
Products: NA art, every kind of NA craftwork, contemporary and traditional

NATIVE RING
Phoenix Indian Center
2601 N 3rd St Ste 100
Phoenix, AZ 85004
520-263-1017
Products: NA community enterprise

PUEBLO GRANDE MUSEUM
4619 E Washington St
Phoenix, AZ 85034
602-495-0901
Products: NA exhibits and presentations, Indian Market, with more than 615 exhibitors/58 tribes

BUFFALO MUSEUM OF AMERICA
Scottsdale, AZ 85253
602-951-1022
Products: A tribute to the buffalo

HOO-HOOGAM KI MUSEUM
Rt 1 Box 216
Sat River Pima-Maricopa Comm
Scottsdale, AZ 85256
602-874-8190
Products: NA exhibits

ANNIE BEARCLOUD
Wild Frontier Auction
PO Box 1011
Sedona, AZ 86339
520-282-0586
Products: Western auctions

* LAKOTA BRAIDING COMPANY
PO Box 172
Sells, AZ 85634-0172
520-383-5517
Brochure/price list: $2
Products: Prorodeo bull ropes, 5, 7, 9 plaits, Block, riser, handholds quarter, half, full, Leather laced

ARIZONA STATE UNIVERSITY POWWOW COMMITTEE
PO Box 248
Tempe, AZ 85280-0248
Products: Sponsors powwows in the Tempe area

ARIZONA STATE MUSEUM
Univ of Arizona
Tucson
AZ 85721
520-679-2231
Products: NA arts and crafts exhibits and presentations

SABINO CANYON RUIN
Tucson, AZ
520-798-1201
Products: Hohokam Indian village site

SAN XAVIER DIST OF THE TOHONO O'ODHAM NATION
2018 W San Xavier Rd
Tucson, AZ 85746
Fax: 520-294-0613
Products: San Xavier District manages a beverage company

* ACORN PRODUCTIONS
Wickenburg, AZ
602-258-5700
Products: Promoters of Western and Indian Show in Wickenburg, Arizona

* KTNN RADIO
PO Box 2569
Window Rock, AZ
86515-2569
Products: NA radio station

NAVAJO NATIONS CORRECTION PROJECT
PO Drawer 709
Window Rock, AZ 86515
Products: Addresses concerns in NA correction facilities

QUECAN MUSEUM
PO Box 11352
Yuma, AZ 85366
619-572-0661
Products: NA exhibits and presentations

CALIFORNIA

SOUTHERN INDIAN HEALTH COUNCIL INC
PO Box 2128
Alpine, CA 91901
619-445-1188
Products: NA health clinic, Substance abuse program

ORIE MEDICINEBULL POWWOW
PO Box 607
Auberry, CA 93602
209-855-2705
Products: Powwow sponsored by Am Ind Women's Assoc, Am Ind Ctr of Ctrl CA, Intertribal Ed Coal

FIRST AMERICANS IN THE ARTS
PO Box 17780
Beverly Hills
CA 90209-3780
310-278-3848
Info: Call
Products: Non-profit trust organization, Native and non-Native professionals in entertainment industry

* New listings, NA = Native American,
SW = Southwest.

**TOIYABE INDIAN
HEALTH PROJECT**
PO Box 1296
Bishop, CA 93515
619-873-8464
Products: NA health
clinic

**N CALIFORNIA
INDIAN
DEVELOPMENT
COUNCIL INC**
241 F St
Eureka, CA 95501-0450
Products: NA commu-
nity organization; jobs
training; cultural events

**SOUTHERN
CALIFORNIA INDIAN
CENTER INC**
PO Box 2550
Garden Grove
CA 92642-2550
714-530-0225
Products: Sponsors "the
largest powwow and
arts and crafts show in
California"

IDYLLWILD ARTS
Summer Program
PO Box 38
Idyllwild, CA 92549
909-659-2171 ext 371
Products: NA art and
culture programs, work-
shops Basketry, drum
making, pottery, more

**CHECKS IN THE
MAIL**
5314 N Irwindale Ave
Irwindale
CA 91706-2003
800-733-4443
Brochure: Free
Products: SW design
bank checks

*** BULLOCK
PRODUCTIONS**
8291 Carburton St
Long Beach
CA 90808-3302
310-430-5112
Products: NA show,
sale, and powwow
schedules in California

*** AMERICAN INDIAN
CULTURE &
RESEARCH JOURNAL**
3220 Campbell Hall
University of California
Los Angeles, CA 90024
Products: American
Indian studies

*** GENE AUTRY
WESTERN HERITAGE
MUSEUM SHOP**
4700 Western Heritage
Way
Los Angeles
CA 90027-1462
213-667-2000 ext 228
Catalog: Available
Products: Western arti-
facts, books on western
subjects

**SOUTHWEST
MUSEUM**
234 Museum Dr
Los Angeles, CA 92101
619-239-2001
Products: NA exhibits
and presentations

**OAKLAND MUSEUM
OF CALIFORNIA**
1000 Oak St
Oakland, CA 94607
510-238-3401
Products: California
Native collections; bas-
kets, weavings, crafts,
carvings, artifacts con-
temp/trad

**SOUTH AND
MESO-AMERICAN
INDIAN INFO
CENTER**
PO Box 28703
Oakland, CA 94604
Products: Addresses
issues in NA country

**AMERICAN INDIAN
TRAINING
INSTITUTE INC**
4221 Northgate Blvd
Ste 2
Sacramento, CA 95834
916-920-0731
Brochure: Free
Products: School for
counselors, health reps,
social workers, educa-
tors, tribal councils,
more

INDIAN DISPUTE SERVICES
Sacramento, CA
916-447-4800
Products: Youth projects; national non-profit American Indian org.

MARY YOUNGBLOOD
5333 Calistoga Way
Sacramento, CA 95841
916-332-4505
Products: Songwriter, poet and talented flutist

SAN DIEGO MUSEUM OF MAN
1350 El Prado
San Diego, CA 92101
619-239-2001
Products: Handwoven textiles, art, sculpture, masks, painting, ritual objects, more

AMERICAN INDIAN MOVEMENT (AIM)
2017 Mission St Rm 303
San Francisco, CA 94103
415-552-1992
Products: Addresses issues in Indian country

INTERNATIONAL INDIAN TREATY COUNCIL
123 Townsend St #575
San Francisco
CA 94107-1907
415-512-1501
Products: Addresses NA problems around the country

PAMELA SHIELDS CARROLL
2408 Folsom St
San Francisco, CA 94110
Products: Photographer of the Blood Indian Reserve Alternative photographic processes

STANFORD AMERICAN INDIAN ORGANIZATION
PO Box 2990
Stanford, CA 94309
415-723-4078
Products: Sponsors of Indian Sobriety pow-wows

COLORADO

* NATIVE AMERICAN RIGHTS FUND
1522 Broadway
Boulder, CO 80302-4296
303-447-8760
Products: Addresses issues in NA country

NATIVE AMERICAN FISH AND WILDLIFE SOCIETY
750 Burbank St
Broomfield, CO 80020
303-466-1725
Products: Fish and wildlife organization Sponsors conferences and other events

AMERICAN INDIAN ANTI DEFAMATION COUNCIL
215 Fifth St
Denver, CO 80204
Products: Addresses issues in NA country

AMERICAN INDIAN HEALTH CARE ASSOCIATION
1999 Broadway Ste 2530
Denver, CO 80202
Products: Association serving urban American Indians, Non profit organization

* COLORADO COMMISSION OF INDIAN AFFAIRS
Rm 130 State Capitol
Denver, CO 80203
Products: NA bureau

---

* New listings, NA = Native American,
SW = Southwest.

COUNCIL OF ENERGY RESOURCE TRIBES
1999 Broadway Ste 2600
Denver, CO 80202
Products: Environmental remediation and environmental protection programs

* NATIONAL URBAN INDIAN COUNCIL
100068 University Park Sta
Denver, CO 80210
Products: National Indian organization for off-reservation Indians

WESTERN AMERICAN INDIAN CHAMBER
1660 17th St #200
Denver, CO 90202
303-620-9292
Products: NA conferences, events

AMERICAN INDIAN DEVELOPMENT FOUNDATION
3030 S College Ave
Ste 202
Fort Collins, CO 80525
303-226-0273
Brochure: Free
Products: Created to benefit NAs through education programs and business assistance

MUSEUM OF WESTERN COLORADO
PO Box 20000
Grand Junction, CO
81502-5020
970-242-0971
Info: Write or call
Products: "Grand River Indian Artists Gathering;" art from contemporary NA artists, more

COLORADO COUNTRY STYLE
2670 E County Line Rd
Highlands Ranch
CO 80126
303-741-5250
Products: Furniture: rustic, country and mountain log, leather, iron, and ceramics; accessories

BUNKY ECHO-HAWK
PO Box 764
Lyons, CO 80540
303-823-5547
Products: NA writer of plays, poetry, fiction, Paints, draws, sculpts

PAWS CHILDRENS MUSEUM
Pueblo Art Works
210 N Santa Fe Ave
Pueblo, CO 81003
719-543-0130
Products: Interactive exhibits that explore the art and culture of various NA tribes

KIRKWELL CATTLE COMPANY
Box 91
Springfield, CO 81090
719-523-4422
Products: Tours through Picture Canyon, and Comanche National Grasslands; horseback/wagons

DISTRICT OF COLUMBIA

AMERICAN INDIAN SOCIETY OF WASHINGTON DC
703-978-8307
Products: NA organization, Sponsors pow-wows,

* MUSEUM OF THE AMERICAN INDIAN
600 Maryland Ave SW
Ste 295
Washington, DC
20024-2520
Products: National NA museum,

* NATIONAL CONGRESS OF AMERICAN INDIANS (NCAI)
900 Pennsylvania Ave SE
Washington, DC
20003-2140
Products: National organization addressing NA issues,

SMITHSONIAN CRAFT SHOW

Smithsonian Institution
A&l 1465, MRC411
Washington, DC 20560
202-357-4000
Info: Send SASE,
Products: Juried exhibitions and sales; calls for entries yearly,

FLORIDA

* FLORIDA GOVERNORS COUNCIL ON INDIAN AFFAIRS
1020 LaFayette St
Ste 102
Tallahassee
FL 32301-4546
Products: Governor's council

AMERICAN INDIAN ASSN OF FLORIDA
PO Box 43
Winter Park, FL 32790
407-952-1541
Products: Sponsors of powwows in Florida

GEORGIA

FESTIVAL OF FIRES
Gwinnett Council for Arts
6400 Sugarloaf Pkwy NW
Duluth, GA
770-623-6002
Products: Educational programs, Fine arts exhibit, drum and dance exhibitions

ILLINOIS

* AMERICAN INDIAN CENTER
1630 W Wilson Ave
Chicago, IL 60640-5418
Products: Community NA center

FIRST NATIONS NATIVE AMERICAN FILM/VIDEO FEST
312-784-0808
Am Ind Econ Dev Assn
Products: Promotes economic development of Am Ind community in the Chicago area

INDIANA

* CIVIL RIGHT COMMISSION
100 N Senate Ave
Rm N 103
Indianapolis
IN 46204-2211
Products: Minority rights bureau

IOWA

CIRCLE OF FIRST NATIONS
IA
515-246-8591
Products: Sponsors powwows in Iowa

KENTUCKY

TRAIL OF TEARS COMMISSION
PO Box 4027
Hopkinsville, KY 42241
502-886-8033
Products: Sponsors powwows in Kentucky

LOUISIANA

* LAFAYETTE NATURAL HISTORICAL MUSEUM
637 Girard Park Drive
LaFayette
LA 70503-2803
Products: NA exhibits

* FRIENDS OF THE CABILLO MUSEUM SHOP
523 Saint Ann Street
New Orleans
LA 70116-3318
Products: Supporters of museum and NA exhibits

* New listings, NA = Native American,
SW = Southwest.

MAINE

ROBERT ABBE MUSEUM OF STONE AGE ANTIQUITIES
Box 286
Bar Harbor, ME
207-288-3519
Products: NA art and crafts

* MAINE INDIAN TRIBAL STATE COMMISSION
PO Box 87
Hallowell
ME 04347-0087
Products: NA bureau

HUDSON MUSEUM
Univ of Maine
Maine Center for the Arts
Orono, ME 04496-5745
602-252-8840/602-252-8848
Products: NA arts and crafts exhibits

MARYLAND

LEAGUE OF INDIGENOUS SOVEREIGN NATIONS
Piscataway Indian Nation
Box 31
Accokeek, MD 20607
301-932-0808
Products: Addresses issues in NA country

MINORITY MEDICAL FACULTY DEVELOPMENT PROGRAM
4733 Bethesda Ave
Ste 350
Bethesda, MD 20814
301-913-0210
Products: Postdoctoral research fellowships to physicians committed to their careers

* MARYLAND COMMISSION ON INDIAN AFFAIRS
100 Community Place
Crownsville
MD 21032-2025
Products: NA bureau

* MINORITY ORGANIZATIONS
Garrett Park Press
PO Box 190
Garrett Park
MD 20896-0190
Products: Publications for minorities

ROY A HARRELL
46 Davis Rd
Street, MD 21154
410-399-0448
Products: Washington, DC American Indian Antiques Show

MASSACHUSETTS

* COMMISSION ON INDIAN AFFAIRS
1 Ashburton Pl Rm 104
Boston, MA 02108-1518
Products: NA bureau

ELDERHOSTEL
Boston, MA
617-426-5437
Info: Call
Products: Educational expeditions, one to British Columbia native village

* HARVARD NATIVE AMERICAN PROGRAM
Harvard University
Read House, Appian Way
Cambridge, MA 0238
Products: NA college program

BENTLEY COLLEGE
Minority Scholars
Waltham MA 02454
800-442-4273
Info: Call
Products: Seven week program for minority students, accountancy practices and careers

MICHIGAN

**COUNTRY
Folk Art Shows Inc**
8393 E Holly Rd
Holly, Ml 48442
810-634-4151
Products: Country decorating folk art shows and sales

*** MICHIGAN
COMMISSION OF
INDIAN AFFAIRS**
PO Box 30026
Lansing, Ml 48909-7526
Products: NA bureau

MINNESOTA

**INDIGENOUS
ENVIRONMENTAL
NETWORK**
PO Box 485
Bemidji, MN 56601
Products: Addresses environmental concerns in NA country

**ANISHINABE LEGAL
SERVICES**
PO Box 157
Cass Lake, MN 56633
Products: NA legal services in local area

**SEVENTH
GENERATION FUND**
RR 1 PO Box 108
Ponsford, MN 56575
218-573-3049
Info: Write
Products: Native nonprofit organizations working on issues of cultural preservation; funds proposals

**MARKETPLACE
PRODUCTIONS**
1885 University Ave
#235
St Paul, MN 55104
612-645-6061
Products: Conferences on NA issues

*** MINNESOTA
INDIAN AFFAIRS
COUNCIL**
127 University Ave
Saint Paul
MN 55155-0001
Products: NA organization

**NATIVE ARTS CIRCLE
Two Rivers Festival**
MN
612-870-7173
Products: Org supports NA artists and educates public about NA art Festival showcases NA works

MISSISSIPPI

* ANCIENT WAYS
2736 Revere St
Jackson, MS 39212
601-373-7692
Flyer: Free
Products: Nonprofit organization, strives to establish better understanding of NA culture to public

MISSOURI

HAIC
1340 E Admiral Blvd
Kansas City, MO 64106
816-421-7608
Products: Non-profit Indian Center

**GEORGE BROWN
SCHOOL OF SOCIAL
WORK**
**Washington University
Campus**
Box 1196
St Louis, MO 63130-4899
Products: Center for Am Ind studies promotes professional education for American Indians

* New listings, NA = Native American,
SW = Southwest.

MONTANA

AMERICAN INDIAN CLUB
Center for Native American Studies
Rm 1 - Wilson Hall MSU
Bozeman, MT 59715
406-994-3751
Products: Sponsors powwows in Montana

GREAT FALLS NA ART ASSOCIATION
2611 S 16th St
Ft Pierce, FL 34982
407-465-2230
Dean and Jacie Davis
Products: Annual Montana SW, Western and Wildlife Marketplace

MONTANA BIG SKY POWWOW COUNCIL
PO Box 6043
Helena, MT 59604
800-654-9085
Products: Sponsors Montana powwows

DEBRA EARLING
336 S 6th W
Missoula, MT 59801
503-934-2134
Products: NA writer

KICKING HORSE JOB CORPS CENTER
Ronan, MT
800-234-5705
Products: Vocational training programs for NAs under the age of 25, Scholarships available

INDIAN LAW RESOURCE CENTER
602 N Ewing
St Helena, MT 59601
406-449-2006
Products: Non-profit advocacy organization providing free legal help to Indian, Alaska Natives

NEBRASKA

* INDIAN AFFAIRS COMMISSION
PO Box 94981
Lincoln, NE 68509-4981
Products: NA bureau

INDIAN CENTER INC
1100 Military Rd
Lincoln, NE 68708
402-438-5231
Products: NA community organization

VERY SPECIAL ARTS
PO Box 163
Norfolk, NE 68702-0163
Products: National photodocumentary project and touring exhibition of disabled NA artisan entries

NEBRASKA INDIAN COMMUNITY COLLEGE
PO Box 752
Winnebago, NE 68071
Products: NA community college

NEW JERSEY

MURIELLE BORST
88 Summit Ave
Jersey City, NJ 07310
201-435-1962
Products: Stand-up NA comedian Dancer with Thunderbird American Indian Dancers

MONTCLAIR ART MUSEUM
3 S Mountain Ave
Montclair, NJ 07042
201-746-5555
Products: NA exhibits and presentations

* ETHNIC ADVISORY COUNCIL
State House CN 101
Trenton, NJ 08625
Products: Governor's Office

NEW MEXICO

ATIIN INC
Native CyberTrade
One Technology Center
1155 University Blvd SE
Albuquerque, NM 87106
505-843-4292
http://www.atiin.com/
cybertrade
Products: NA internet
site, features arts and
crafts, associations, businesses

GATHERING OF NATIONS
PO Box 75102
Albuquerque, NM 87194
800-551-6291
Products: Largest powwow in North America;
Miss Indian World contest, Int'l world celebration

* MAXWELL MUSEUM OF ANTHROPOLOGY
University of NM campus
University Blvd
Albuquerque
NM 87131-0001
505-277-4404
Products: Cultural displays, and public programs

STAR HORSE COMMUNICATIONS
Powwow Hotline
Albuquerque, NM
900-4-POWWOW
Products: Recorded
phone msgs, powwow
listing, Fundraiser for
Gathering of Nations
Powwow

NEW MEXICO SCHOOL FOR VISUALLY HANDICAPPED
1900 North White Sands
Alamogordo, NM 88310
505-439-4490
Products: Institute
which has some Native
American residents

INTER-TRIBAL INDIAN CEREMONIAL
PO Box 1
Church Rock, NM 87311
Products: NA organization

DEMING LUNA MIMBRES MUSEUM
321 S Silver
Deming, NM 88030
505-546-2382
Products: NA museum

PUYE CLIFF DWELLINGS
Santa Clara Pueblo
PO Box 580
Espanola, NM 87532
505-599-1197
Products: NA cultural site

SANDSTONE PRODUCTIONS
901 N Fairgrounds Rd
Farmington, NM 87401
505-599-1197
Products: Native New
Mexico enterprise

BANDELIER NATIONAL MONUMENT
HCR 1 Box 1 Ste 15
Los Alamos, NM 87544
505-672-3861
Products: NA monument site

INN OF THE MOUNTAIN GODS
Mescalero Apache Res
PO Box 269
Mescalero, NM 88340
800-545-9011
Products: Reservation
enterprise

CHACO CULTURE NATIONAL HISTORIC PARK
PO Box 220
Nageezi
NM 87037-0220
505-786-7014
Products: NA cultural
site

* New listings, NA = Native American,
SW = Southwest.

**PECOS NATIONAL
HISTORICAL PARK**
PO Box 418
Pecos, NM 87552
505-757-6414
Products: NA cultural
site

*** GADOHI
USQUANIGODI INC**
PO Box 1810
Rancho De Taos
NM 87557
Products: Non profit
organization; NA video

*** RT COMPUTER
GRAPHICS INC**
602 San Juan de Rio
Rio Rancho
NM 87124-1146
505-891-1600
Products: NA computer
graphics programs,
Plains/Southwest style

**NATIVE AMERICAN
PREPARATORY
SCHOOL**
PO Box 160
Rowe, NM 87562-0160
505-474-2270/505-421-2770
Products: Residential
learning experience for
gifted NA students
entering the 9th and
10th grades

**EIGHT NORTHERN
INDIAN PUEBLOS
Artist/Craftsmen Show**
Santa Clara Pueblo NM
505-852-4265
Products: 480 artists
exhibit; food, dancing,
footraces, events, other
activities, usually in July

HOTEL SANTA FE
1501 Paseode Peralta
Santa Fe, NM 87501
800-825-9876
Products: NA-owned
hotel

**MUSEUM OF INDIAN
ARTS AND CULTURE**
708 Camino Lejo
Santa Fe, NM 87501
505-827-6334
Products: SW pottery,
NA art and crafts, con-
temporary/traditional;
textiles, dolls, baskets,
silverwork

**NEW MEXICO STATE
MONUMENTS**
PO Box 2087
Santa Fe, NM 87504
505-827-6334
Products: NA cultural
sites info

*** PUEBLO POEH
MUSEUM**
Rt 11 Box 27-E
Santa Fe, NM 97501
505-455-2489
Products: Pueblo arti-
facts, crafts, textiles,
clothing, blankets, more

**RECURSOS OF
SANTA FE**
826 Camino de Monte
Rey Ste 43
Santa Fe, NM 87505-3961
505-438-3185
Flyers: Free
Products: Non profit
org which expands sales
of NM businesses
Supports NA direct
trade activities

**RED NATION
CELEBRATION**
Santa Fe during Indian
Market, summer
505-474-4770
Products: Concerts,
inaugural show featur-
ing artists such as
Robert Mirabal, Litefoot,
Am Ind Theater

**SCHOOL OF
AMERICAN
RESEARCH**
660 Garcia St
Santa Fe, NM 87501
505-982-3584
Products: NA cultural
research

**SW ASSN FOR
INDIAN ARTS**
Santa Fe Indian Mkt
509 Camino de los
Marquez Ste 1
Santa Fe, NM 87501
505-983-5220
Summer event
Products: Many events,
film festival, NA artist
showcase, food, demon-
strations, presentations

**GILA CLIFF
DWELLINGS
NATIONAL
MONUMENT**
Rt 11 Box 100
Silver City, NM 87401
505-536-9461
Products: Ancient NA
cultural site

**GERONIMO SPRINGS
MUSEUM**
211 Main St
Truth or Consequences
NM 87901
505-894-6600
Products: NA artifacts

NEW YORK

*** AMERICAN
MUSEUM OF NAT'L
HISTORY MUSEUM
GIFT SHOP**
Central Park at 79th St
New York, NY 10024
Products: Carries NA
products, has museum
exhibits

*** ASSOCIATION ON
AMERICAN INDIAN
AFFAIRS INC**
245 Fifth Ave
New York, NY 10016
Products: Addresses
issues in NA country

**FILM AND VIDEO
CENTER**
**Nat'l Museum of the
American Indian**
One Bowling Green
New York, NY 10004
212-825-6914
Products: International
films, video and radio
festivals of indigenous
communities

**NAT'L MUSEUM OF
THE AMERICAN
INDIAN**
George Gustav Heye
Center
One Bowling Green
New York, NY 10004
212-825-6992
Products: NA museum;
presentations, exhibits,
extensive collection of
NA items

**SPIDERWOMAN
THEATER**
425 W 23rd St Ste 1 E
New York, NY 10011
212-691-1970
Liz Dunn
Products: NA women's
traveling theater group

*** WBAI PACIFICA
RADIO 99.5 FM 505**
8th Ave
New York, NY 10018
212-279-0707 ext 121
No catalog
Products: Radio pro-
gramming focusing on
NA politics, history, and
culture, airs 9 pm east-
ern

*** NATIVE AMERICAN
CENTER FOR THE
LIVING ARTS INC**
PO Box 945
Niagara Falls, NY 14302
Products: NA items

NORTH
CAROLINA

KITUWAH
PO Box 2854
Asheville, NC 28802
704-254-0072
Products: American
Indian celebration of
arts, heritage, and edu-
cation

**MUSEUM OF THE
CHEROKEE INDIAN**
PO Box 1599
Cherokee, NC 28719
704-497-3481
Products: Cherokee
museum

* New listings, NA = Native American,
SW = Southwest.

NORTH DAKOTA

UNITED TRIBES INT POWWOW
United Tribes Tech College
3315 University Dr
Bismarck, ND 58504
701-255-3285
Products: College sponsors NA powwows, art expos, conferences, sports tournaments, dances, more

PRAIRIE MEDIATION & CONSULTING
1395 S Columbia Rd
Ste 319
Grand Forks
ND 58201-4011
701-780-9732
Info: Free
Products: For a fee, finds funding sources for minority businesses

RAIN PROGRAM
PO Box 9025
Grand Forks
ND 59202-9025
701-777-3224
Products: Health education/nurse aide certification programs, Hosted

* COMMISSION ON INDIAN AFFAIRS
325 N Salisbury St, Ste 579
Raleigh, NC 27603-1388
Products: NA bureau

OHIO

* NATIVE AMERICAN INDIAN CENTER, THE
756 Parsons Ave
Columbus, OH 43207
614-443-6120
Products: Serves social/cultural needs of NA community in central Ohio

OKLAHOMA

* CHICKASAW HISTORICAL SOCIETY
PO Box 1548
Ada, OK 74821-1548
Products: Chickasaw tribal society

FIVE CIVILIZED TRIBES MUSEUM
Agency Hill on Honor Hts Dr
Muskogee, OK 74401
918-683-1701
Products: NA museum, Publishes a newsletter

NATIONAL POWWOW
933 Bradley
Oklahoma City
OK 73127
Products: Powwow info

CENTER FOR LOCAL GOVERNMENT TECH
308 CITD
Stillwater, OK 74078
Products: Provides training and tech assistance to tribal members in transportation-related field

OKLAHOMA NATIVE AMERICAN BUSINESS DEVELOP CTR
2727 E 21st St Ste 102
Tulsa, OK 74114
918-743-1115
Products: Offers tech assistance in area of procurement packages for business loans and bonding

PHILBROOK MUSEUM OF ART
2727 S Rockford Rd
Tulsa, OK 74152-0510
918-749-7941
Products: NA art exhibits

TULSA INDIAN ART FESTIVAL
PO Box 52694
Tulsa, OK 74152-0694
918-838-3875
Affiliate, Nat'l Ind Monument/lnst
Products: Volunteer network sponsors performing and visual arts scholarships

OREGON

HIGH DESERT MUSEUM, THE
59800 S Hwy 97
Bend, OR 97702
541-382-4754
Products: NA artifacts, traditional and contemporary SW jewelry, Navajo blankets, roaches, dress

* CELILO WYAM INDIAN COMMUNITY
PO Box 323
The Dalles
OR 97058-0323
Products: Native American community at Columbia River

EAGLE FEATHER CONSTRUCTION INC
25325 Grand Ronde Rd
Grand Ronde, OR 97347
541-879-5346
Products:
Residential/commercial remodeling, additions, decks, Local area

KLAMATH DRUG AND ALCOHOL ABUSE PROGRAM
310 S 5th St
Klamath Falls
OR 97601-6108
Products: NA alcohol /drug treatment programs

KLAMATH KOWBOY KORRAL
2508½ Altamont Dr
Klamath Falls
OR 97603-5702
541-882-0212
Products: Rodeo gear; chaps, belts, purses; repair work Native-owned

SPOTTED HORSE TRIBAL GIFTS
Diane McAlister
PO Box 869
Oakridge
OR 97463-0869
Catalog: $2
Products: NA merchandise, art; Cherokee Research; books; Native American perfumes and soaps

* ATNI NEWSLETTER
324 NE 20th Ave Ste 310
Portland, OR 97232
Products: NA publication

* CONCERNED INDIAN COMMITTEE
6008 N Syracuse St
Portland, OR 97203-5150
Products: Community NA organization

INDIAN ED ACT PROGRAM
Portland Public Schools
8020 Tillimook St
Portland, OR 97213-6655
Products: Indian education office

* INDIAN WORLD
20 SE 8th Ave
Portland, OR 97214-1203
Products: KBOO Radio FM

* NATIVE AMERICAN ART COUNCIL PORTLAND ART MUSEUM
1219 Park Ave
Portland, OR 97205-2430
Products: Sponsors NA artists

TECH MATIC
3727 SE Knapp
Portland, OR 97202
503-774-4400
Products: Contract video/electronic services, computer upgrades, consulting, video production, satellites

---

* New listings, NA = Native American, SW = Southwest.

* AFFIRMATIVE ACTION OFFICE
775 Court St NE
Salem, OR 97310-0001
Products: NA affirmative action office

* CHEMAWA INDIAN SCHOOL
3700 Chemawa Rd NE
Salem, OR 97305-1119
541-399-5721
ext 226/228/222
Products: NA educational institution

DEPT OF EDUCATION
700 Pringle Pkwy SE
Salem, OR 97310-0001
Products: Indian education/civil rights

* INIPI OYATE KI INDIAN CULTURE CLUB
2405 Deer Park Dr SE
Salem, OR 97310-9302
Products: Oregon State Correctional facility, inmates club

LAKOTA OYATE KI INDIAN CULTURE CLUB
2605 State St
Salem, OR 97310-1346
Products: Oregon State Penitentiary, NA inmate club

* LEGISLATIVE COMMISSION ON INDIAN AFFAIRS
454 State Capitol
Salem, OR 97310-0001
Products: NA bureau

NATIONAL INDIAN ATHLETIC ASSOCIATION
4084 Ibex NE
Salem, OR 97305
541-390-4245
Info: Call or write
Products: Promoting sports education for youth, fighting substance abuse, suicide, dropouts, etc

* OREGON ARTS COMMISSION
775 Summer St NE
Salem, OR 97310-1364
Products: Arts organization, assistance available for NA artisans

SPIRIT COMMUNICATIONS INC
20493 SW Avery Ct
Tualatin, OR 97602
541-612-0600
Products: Voice and data co implementing networks for tomorrow

KAH-NEE-TA RESORT
Warm Springs Reservation
PO Box K
Warm Springs
OR 97761-3000
800-554-4786
Brochure: Free
Products: Full service resort featuring NA foods, cultural events Owned/operated by Confed Tribes

STEVE BOBB GRAPHICS
Design and Manufacturing
PO Box 99
Willamina, OR 97396
541-876-3118
Products: Creative artwork for cars, trucks, signs, shirts

SOUTH DAKOTA

* DACOTAH PRAIRIE MUSEUM
21 S Main St
Aberdeen SD 57401-4218
Products: NA art, crafts, exhibits

NORTHERN PLAINS HEALTHY START PROJECT
405 8th Ave NW Ste 305
Aberdeen, SD 57401
605-229-3515
Products: Project committed to reducing infant deaths in the Aberdeen area

SDABBE
Support Services
PO Box 109
Batesland, SD 57716
605-288-1921
Products: NA conferences; parent training, teacher seminars, proposal and facilities development

* AKTA LAKOTA MUSEUM
St Josephs Indian School
1100 N Jaspar
Chamberlain, SD 57325
605-734-3455
Products: NA art and crafts

DAKOTA INDIAN FOUNDATION
PO Box 340
Chamberlain
SD 57325-0340
Products: Nonprofit corporation funding groups related to social enhancement, development

* FOUR WINDS CULTURAL CENTER
1000 N Crescent St
Flandreau
SD 57028-1221
Products: NA cultural organization

* PONY TRACKS
100 E 2nd Ave
Flandreau
SD 57028-1223
605-997-5284
Products: Custom made saddles, boots, repair, rodeo equipment; Native craftspersons

SWIFT HORSE LODGE
PO Box 157
Fort Thompson, SD 57339
605-245-2245
Products: Crow Creek Sioux alcoholism program

SIOUX SAN ALCOHOLISM PROGRAM
Hope Lodge, SD
605-342-8925
Products: NA alcoholism treatment program

ANPETU LUTA OTIPI
PO Box 275
Kyle, SD 57752
605-455-2331
Products: Assisting NAs in their battle against alcoholism and drug addictions Youth organization

LAKOTA FUND, THE
PO Box 340
Kyle, SD 57752
605-455-2500
Products: NA organization

LOWER BRULE SIOUX TRIBAL TOURISM OFFICE
605-473-5506
Products: Promotes and enhances tourism for economic development and growth in SD NA communities

WESTERN HERITAGE INSURANCE AGENCY
PO Box C
Martin, SD 57551
605-685-6350
Products: NA-owned insurance agency

HIGHER EDUCATION GRANT PROGRAM
Oglala Sioux Tribe
PO Box 562
Pine Ridge
SD 57770-0562
800-832-3651
Products: Educational grants for NA students

* New listings, NA = Native American, SW = Southwest.

PROJECT TAKOJA
SD
605-341-3339/605-343-8762
Products: Culturally relevant support services for pregnant Native American teens

LAKOTA TIMES FOUNDATION
PO Box 2180
Rapid City, SD 57709
605-341-0011
Products; Assists NAs pursuing careers in the field of journalism

RAPID CITY INDIAN HEALTH BOARD
PO Box 1608
Rapid City, SD 57709
Products: NA health organization

SACRED HILLS TREATMENT CENTER
2465 W Chicago St
Rapid City, SD 57702
605-341-9779
Products: NA drug and alcohol treatment center

* OYATE NETWORKING PROJECT INC
West 1st St Box 610
Rosebud, SD 57570
605-747-5311
Products: Lakota organization

ASSOCIATION ON INDIAN AFFAIRS
PO Box 268
Sisseton, SD 57262-0268
Products: NA organization

* DAKOTA NATION BROADCASTING
PO Box 142
Sisseton, SD 57262-0142
Products: NA FM radio

KINI FM STEREO RADIO 96.1
Box 499
St Francis, SD 57572
605-747-2291
Products: NA radio station

* BEAR BUTTE INFORMATION CENTER
PO Box 688
Sturgis, SD 57785-0688
Products: Information about the Bear Butte site in South Dakota

TENNESSEE

CHUCALISSA MUSEUM
University of Memphis
Memphis, TN 38109
901-785-3160
Products: Dept of Anthropology at Museum presents NA exhibits

INDIAN HERITAGE COUNCIL
Box 2302
Morristown, TN 37816
651-581-5714
Products: Promotes deeper understanding between Indians and non Indians; research, education

TEXAS

FRANKS PROMOTIONS
Susan Franks
PO Box 9326
Austin, TX 78766
512-258-7025
Products: American Antique Cowboy and Indian Relics Show

* AMERICAN INDIAN ARTS COUNCIL
725 Preston Royale Shopping Ctr, Ste B
Dallas, TX 75230-3837
Products: NA art organization

TODD BRONCY
Indian Hobbyist
601 N Adams
San Angelo
TX 76901-1704
915-659-4305
Products: Indian hobbyist activities

VIRGINIA

* NATIONAL INDIAN EDUCATION ASSN AIHEC-P
121 Oronoco St
Alexandria
VA 22314-2015
Products: Indian education organization

* INTERNATIONAL BROTHERHOOD DAYS INC
6425 John Jackson Ct
Fairfax Station
VA 22039-1234
703-764-1953
Products: Annual educational work shops, powwows, other events

WORDCRAFT CIRCLE
Moccasin Telegraph
2951 Ellenwood Dr
Fairfax, VA 22031-2038
703-280-1028
Products: Writer's support organization for NAs Membership includes newsletter

* AMERICAN INDIAN ECONOMIC DEVELOPMENT ASSOCIATION
Fredericksburg
VA 22408-7326
Products: NA business organization

WASHINGTON

* NORTHWEST INDIAN COLLEGE
2522 Kwina Rd
Bellingham
WA 98226-9278
360-676-2772
Products: NA Indian college

TRIBAL LEGAL COURSES
7239 E Mercer Way
Mercer Island
WA 98040
206-232-4235
Products: National courses and on site seminars for tribal councils and tribal staffs; legal laws

GOVERNORS OFFICE OF INDIAN AFFAIRS
PO Box 40909
Olympia
WA 98504-0909
Products: NA bureau

* BURKE MUSEUM SHOP
University of Washington DB1
Seattle, WA 98195-0001
Products: Indian art, crafts, info

WISCONSIN

WARRINGTON BUILDERS
Native American Const, Co,
PO Box 790
Keshena, Wl 54135
715-799-4978
Products: Commercial, residential, remodeling firm,

WYOMING

CODY RODEO COMPANY
1291 Sheridan Ave
Cody, WY 82414
Catalog: Free
Products: Cody shopping, rodeos, tickets,

OLD WEST SHOW AND AUCTION
PO Box 655
Cody, WY 82414
307-587-9014
Products: Cowboy collectibles, antiques, western events,

WIND RIVER ASSOCIATES
PO Box 187 Fort
Washakie, WY 82514
307-332-5437/0175
Products: NA seminars, Indian issues,

* New listings, NA = Native American, SW = Southwest.

CANADA

* WESTERN HERITAGE CENTRE
Box 1477
105 River Ave
Cochrane, Alberta
Canada T0L 0W0
403-932-3514
Products: Western ranching, rodeo, agriculture items; Canadian Rodeo Hall of Fame; retail area,

CONFEDERACY OF TREATY 6 FIRST NATIONS
Ste 350, 10621-100 Ave
Edmonton, Alberta
Canada T5J 0B3
Products: Sponsors Aboriginal Youth Conferences, educational

NATIVE INDIAN INUIT PHOTOGRAPHERS ASSN
134 James St S
Hamilton, Ontario
Canada L8P 2Z4
905-529-7477
Products: Membership promoting image of Native and Inuit people through medium of photography,

ROYAL ONTARIO MUSEUM
100 Queens Park
Toronto, Ontario
Canada M5S 2C6
416-586-8000
Products: Displays of NA culture, ancestral teachings, spiritual heritage; contemp/trad artifacts,

Books, Newsletters, Cards, Audio, Videos

Contemporary Crafts and Southwestern Home Accessories

Fine Art, Galleries, Collectibles, Antiques

Finished Jewelry and Silverwork

Foods, Seeds, Herbs, Botanicals

Leather, Leather Goods, Furs, Skulls, Horns

Native American and Southwestern Clothing

Native American Craftmaking Supplies

Native American Organizations, Services, and Miscellaneous

Southwest Furniture, Woodwork

Textilex, Rugs, Blankets

Traditional Native American Arts and Crafts

Diane McAlister, known as Standing-On-A-Star Woman in Native American communities, is of Creek Heritage. She owns Spotted Horse Tribal Gifts, a mail order business based in Oakridge Oregon. She lives a traditional Native life-style with husband Doug, a wildlife biologist in the Diamond Peak Wilderness in Oregon. They are both accomplished craftpersons.

These fine Native American books are available from your local bookstore.

A Basic Call to Consciousness $7.95
America Indian Coloring Book 3.50
Arts & Crafts of the Cherokee 9.95
Aunt Mary Tell Me a Story 3.95
Blackfoot Craftworker's Book .11.95
Chants and Prayers 9.95
Cherokee A B C Coloring Book 3.50
Cherokee Legends and the Trail of Tears 3.95
Cherokee Plants 3.95
The Cherokees Past & Present 3.95
Children of the Circle 9.95
Daughters of Abya Yala 8.95
Dream Feather 11.95
Eyes of Chief Seattle 16.95
Finger Weaving: Indian Braiding 4.95
A Good Medicine Collection: Life in Harmony with Nature 10.95
A Guide to Native American Music Recordings 12.95
How Can One Sell the Air? Chief Seattle's Vision (Revised) . .6.95
How to Make Cherokee Clothing 23.95
Indian Tribes of the Northern Rockies 9.95
Legends Told by the Old People .5.95
Native American Crafts Directory 8.95
A Natural Education 8.95
The People: Native American Thoughts and Feelings 5.95
The Powwow Calendar 8.95
The Pow Wow Trail 8.95
Sacred Song of the Hermit Thrush 5.95
Seven Clans of the Cherokee Society 3.95
Song of the Seven Herbs 11.95
Song of the Wild Violets 5.95
Spirit of the White Bison 5.95
Story of the Cherokee People 3.95
Teachings of Nature 8.95
Traditional Dress 6.95
Where Legends Live 5.95

Also available from:
BOOK PUBLISHING COMPANY
PO BOX 99
Summertown TN 38483
Please include $2.50 per book additional for shipping.

If you are interested in other fine books on Native Americans, ecology, alternative health, gardening, vegetarian cooking and children's books, please call for a free catalog:

1-800-695-2241